Robin Jones and Ian Stewart

# TIMEX SINCLAIR 1000

## Programs, Games and Graphics

BIRKHÄUSER
Boston · Basel · Stuttgart

This is the US edition of the British publication, 'Peek, Poke, Byte & Ram: Program Guide for the Sinclair ZX81', which was published by Shiva Publishing Ltd. This US edition has been adapted to the American market, taking into account new developments in technology and current references.
This edition is available in the US, Canada and Mexico.

Second printing December 1982

Library of Congress in Publication Data

Jones, Robin.
Timex Sinclair 1000.

Includes index.
1. Sinclair ZX81 (Computer)—Programming.
2. Basic (Computer program language)
I. Stewart, Ian. II. Title.
QA76.8.S625J66 001.64′2 82-1291
ISBN 3-7643-3080-5 (Switzerland) AACR2


ISBN 3-7643-3080-5
Printed in USA

# CONTENTS

# APROPOS

This book is a clear, concise guide to Sinclair BASIC, the computer language used by the Timex/Sinclair 1000 and the Sinclair ZX81. Each of its twenty-six chapters—written with the new user in mind—engages the reader interactively in exploring the BASIC commands and related programming techniques.

Although easy to read, this book is not simplistic: it is as useful to an engineer as it is comprehensible to a bright thirteen year old.

We hope that you enjoy this sparkling introduction to the computer experience.

—Birkhäuser Boston, Inc.

# CHIPS THAT PASS IN THE NIGHT?

A small number of inventions have molded much of human history. When Ug the Caveman discovered The Wheel, and his wife Snug invented Fire, they only dimly perceived that they had started *Homo sapiens* on a way of life. We've been at it ever since: the bow and arrow, the plough, the horse as transport, the water-wheel, the steam engine, the automatic loom (those two brought about the first Industrial Revolution), the automobile, the airplane, radio . . .

Now we've managed to invent the microchip (and, some commentators insist, put ourselves out of a job). This, it is said, is the Age of the Computer.

In the early 1950s, how many computers were there? You could count them on the fingers of one hand. Literally: there were four.

Soon—if not already, it depends on how you define "computer"—there will be four million.

It is said that when Tom Watson of IBM first heard about electronic computers he estimated that the requirements of the entire USA could be served by . . . three of them. It hasn't quite worked out that way: nobody could foresee in detail the amazing explosion of information technology that ensued. The Age of the Computer is now 30 years old, and we're going to have to live with it for the rest of our lives, whether we like it or not.

There aren't just more of them: they're smaller, and faster, and more reliable. In 1963 Cambridge University's EDSAC, of which it was justifiably proud, was a block of electronic circuitry (valves, mostly) about the size of a Ford van, and much less reliable—it broke down several times a day. By 1966 it had become obsolete: valves were out, transistors in. Then transistors gave way to integrated circuits and the ubiquitous microchip. Today the Timex/Sinclair 1000 is the size of a cigar-box, retails at $99.95, and can do everything EDSAC did and more.

And the computer is no longer confined to the academic and industrial worlds. It has invaded the home. There are probably more types of Home Computer on the market than there are brands of beer. They range in price from $79.95 (in kit form) to $5000 depending on what facilities you want and how much you want to pay for pretty styling. (Lots of expensive "business micros" are home-computer mutton dressed up as office-sleek lamb, at three times the price.)

This book is about one of them: the aforementioned Timex/ Sinclair 1000, brainchild of "Uncle Clive" Sinclair.

Why concentrate on the 1000? Let's be frank: it's not the most sophisticated machine on the market. In fact, some of its features—such as the touch-sensitive keyboard—require a definite amount of patience to live with. But what do you expect for the price? Artoo-Deetoo? The 1000 represents quite remarkable value for the money. It brings Home Computing within reach of anyone who is prepared to spend the price of a used lawn-mower. The personal computer is no longer the province of a small coterie of enthusiasts: it has gone public. And, while the Timex/Sinclair 1000 has some limitations, it also has most of the features that make computers what they are.

This makes it an ideal machine for *getting started.* Do I really want a personal computer? Will I get bored with it? Will I be able to do anything with it when I get it? With the 1000 you can dip your toe into the turbid microwaters with the minimum of financial risk.

And there are going to be an awful lot of 1000s bought so that the *kids* can dip their toes. (And Dad, of course, will keep a firm parental eye on them while just, errr, finding out how to work the thing in case they need help . . . Ten to one the kids know more about computing than Dad within six months.)

That's fine—to live with the computer you've got to learn to love it, and that means using it, making it do the tricks you want it to—but . . . There's a snag. Time and effort don't matter so much: they're expendable. Dad will just have to visit the pub or the golfcourse less. The need for the domestic TV as a computer monitor requires careful scheduling, nothing more.

No, the problem is that computer programming is extremely

frustrating when you get started. You realize just how *stupid* that silly machine is. It cuts the wondrous micro down to cigar-box-brain size. For example, you tell it to plot a graph and by accident some of the points being plotted go off the edge of the screen. Now, any intelligent being would take that in its stride; but the micro throws a fit, and the program crashes. (Jargon: stops and has to be restarted by you. See, you've learned something already and this is only the introduction.) Or you've laboriously entered a long program, pushed "run", and it doesn't do what you expect; and now the problem is to find out *why*. This is seldom a computer fault; it's a "bug" in the program, an error on *your* part. It can be a desperate task finding it unless you're systematic.

Some people try to avoid all these problems by buying predigested programs on cassette. But that way you'll never learn anything at all about computers. You've *got* to get your hands dirty. Any fool can plug someone else's tape into a machine and push buttons; the interesting task—and the one that starts you towards a skill that could prove very valuable in the future—is *designing* your own programs. (And you'd be surprised how many prepacked programs have bugs, which you'll have to fix anyway.)

The aim of this book is to help you get started. There are a lot of books about microcomputers. There are a small number on the Sinclair Basic. There are very few indeed aimed at the genuine beginner—someone who not only doesn't know what a priority code or a string-handling facility is, but who's not even sure yet how the keyboard works. Even the Timex *Manual*, which comes with the machine, has so much to tell you about that it can only make a few concessions.

So we've put together a very gentle introduction to *some* of the most basic features of the 1000. By the time you've read this book, the *Manual* will hold no terrors. We've included sections on setting up the machine, saving programs on tape, BASIC programming, debugging, number-crunching, and graphics. We've tried to pass on as many useful (and non-esoteric) tips as we can along the way. In addition there are program listings: if you've nothing better to do you can copy these into the machine and see what happens, although we hope you'll take them to bits to see how they tick. To test your grasp of the jargon there's a special T/S-crossword; and "De Bugs" will keep you amused when attention is flagging. Everything is designed to run on the unexpanded 1K ZX81—the basic machine without the expanded memory.

We've also tried to break everything down into digestible pieces, so that you have a chance of spending a couple of hours on the machine and coming away having achieved something definite.

Lots of computer books give the impression they're trying to prove how clever their authors are. We're not doing that: everything here is very straightforward and basic. We think that's what an *introduction* to the world of the computer ought to look like. The hardest part is getting off the ground.

> So far, we've referred to ourselves collectively as "we", but this won't work very well later. Personal experiences relayed by a "we" take on a curious air. Since any given section was written by only one of us, we have plumped for the word "I" to describe us both. If that disturbs you, consider how often a singular author refers to himself as "we"!

If you have successfully set up a 1000 and got it working, you won't need to read this. If you haven't, it may save you having to launder the cat.

# UP AND RUNNING

It nestled shiny and inscrutable in its expanded polystyrene cradle, protected even against those parcel-mugging thugs in the post office. My Timex/Sinclair 1000! Megabytes of computing power at the touch of an elbow, or whatever.

Having unpacked it, the next step was to connect it up to the TV. If you don't do this it still works, but you have no idea what it's actually up to—which is distressing if, like me, you're prone to microparanoia (the ingrained suspicion that microcomputers are trying to take over the world). Now, I know that of course, Timex's *Manual* tells you exactly what to do, in easyread type of crystalline clarity, but . . . experience acquired in the field is always valuable, hence this offering of expert advice.

Are you sitting comfortably? Good. (That's not just idle chit-chat, as you'll appreciate after your first two-hour session of kneeling on the floor by the TV.)

Now, take the transformer—the black box that looks like an overfed electric plug. Attached to it, on a long wire, is a little black jackplug. Disentangle this from the cat, which has been playing with it while you've been perusing this masterpiece of literature, and push the plug sharp end foremost into the socket on the 1000 marked "9V DC in." That's 9 volts of Direct Current, and has nothing whatsoever to do with airplanes.

Plug the prongs of the transformer into the wall plug, close enough to the TV for the wires to reach.

Next, find the switch box. If it's not there, X-ray the cat before complaining to Timex. It's a box a little smaller than a cigarette pack. There is a switch on top marked GAME and TV. Disconnect the VHF antenna leads from your TV and connect them to the two screws marked "connect to antenna;" now connect the wires on the TV from which you just finished removing the antenna leads. Finally, find the cord with two plugs on it; plug one end into the jack marked TV on the 1000 and the other end to the game jack on the switch box.

Make sure the TV is plugged in—*don't* unplug the transformer, you need two sockets or a two-way extension thingy. If your sockets have switches, turn them on.

The next step is essential. *Turn the volume control right down.* If not, Granny will have hysterics, the cat will disappear up the chimney covering the furniture with soot, and . . . Be warned, the world is a cruel place for the Single Programmer with a hungry Micro to feed.

Now turn the TV on.

If you see dim, moving pictures (Figure 1), you left the set tuned to Channel 56 last night. The 1000 may or may not enjoy watching this—it's a deep philosophical question which no 1000 has ever been willing to answer to human satisfaction—but it will only talk to you if you tune in to the right channel.

If your set is one of those that have a numbered dial for VHF channels, turn it to Channel 2: go raid the refridgerator. On no account use Channel No. 5—it stinks. (Joke.) If you don't like Channel 2 try Channel 3, there is a little switch on the bottom of your 1000 that gives you the choice.

Start adjusting the VHF fine tuner and watch the screen changing. You'll probably see a darkish background with random white speckles, like an insane ants' nest or an aerial view of Tokyo at night. (At this stage, you can turn the volume up *very*

Figure 1
No, you've left it tuned
to Channel 56

gently; you'll see why I told you to turn it down. It hisses something dreadful. This is a normal habit of TV sets and is not Timex's fault.)

Turn that tuner. If you reach the end and nothing has happened, turn it the *other* way. When you get near the right place you'll see some rather formless, flickering smudges down the left side of the screen. Turn gently, a bit more; you should now see a tiny square near the bottom left corner (Figure 2).

It's actually an inverse video K—that is, a white K on a black square—but unless you've been lucky, you won't see it very clearly. Adjust the brightness and contrast controls on the TV until it is as legible as you can manage—a grey background, not too bright, with a crisp little square whose "K" stands out clearly (Figure 3). If you get some other junk instead of "K"

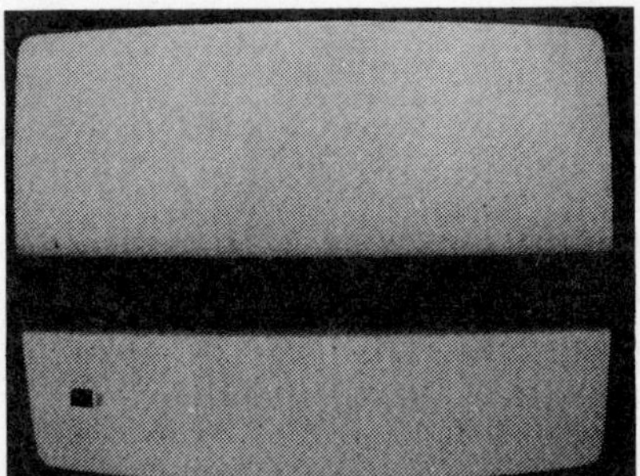

Figure 2 Nearly there . . .

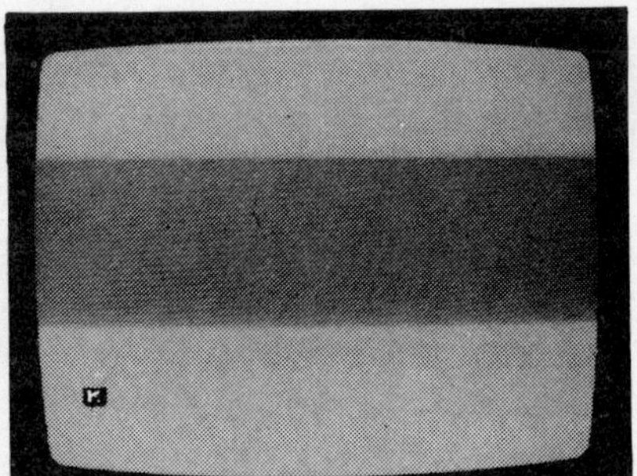

Figure 3 Perfect!

you've accidentally touched the 1000 keyboard, so press "SHIFT" with one finger and "DELETE" with the other until it disappears and the "K" comes back. If you have to, turn the color control right down to black and white.

If you still don't like the clarity, try screwing the various plugs gently into their sockets to make better contact. If nothing remotely like what I've been describing is happening, you can test the TV connection lead for continuity or short-circuits using a battery and a flashlight bulb (see page 53); and you can test the output from the DC adaptor (but use a 9V bulb or you'll blow it). If it still won't work, send it back and try again.

If all is well, try pressing some keys on the 1000 keyboard. Unlike typewriter keys, these work by detecting the pressure of your fingers, and you don't feel much "give" when you push; but you should see words and letters coming up on the screen. Now you're ready to read the *Manual* and start computing. If you can't get rid of the junk you've typed in, momentarily disconnect the "9 V DC in" plug. Or get rid of it all by repeated use of DELETE; or—better—hit EDIT (shifted 1) and then ENTER.

Experiment for a bit, and try to get the feel of the keyboard. Nothing you type in can do any harm. If you get stuck, just unplug the power supply and plug it in again, as before.

The first time I set the machine up I was very careful to plug everything in before switching on; but it doesn't really matter much as long as it all goes in the right places. It's hard to electrocute yourself on 9 volts. Timex say it won't damage the 1000 if you accidentally connect the jackplugs to the wrong holes; but of course you must take care with the transformer plug and sockets.

When you switch off, leave the fine tuner as it is and flick the switch box back to TV. Now that's done, tell the kids, Granny, and the cat that Channel 2 (or whatever) is the 1000, so don't fiddle with it. From now on, you only need retune brightness and contrast. It's good public relations to retune these, and the color, back to NBC, when you finish computing. Otherwise, other users of what you have come to think of as your computer monitor will complain that the pictures have been ruined.



Setting up the 1000 is so easy that even the cat could do it; but there's also another item of hardware that is distinctly more tricky: using a cassette recorder to SAVE and LOAD programs on tape. You may want to check these features out straight away. In this case, turn to page 45 for more helpful advice. Ignore the articles in between—they aren't needed for that purpose. I could have put that article next—but two "hardware" items in succession lacks variety, and anyway, the next really important job is to get started on *writing programs*—our main objective.

Even if you've never seen a computer before in your life, you can start programming right away. Program first, ask questions later!

# PREPACKED PROGRAMS

At the end of this book you will find a number of program listings, starting on page 123. *You should feel free at any time to copy out one of these listings and run it,* whether or not you understand the commands contained in the program. All you do is type out the listing on the keyboard, check carefully to make sure there are no mistakes, and press RUN followed by ENTER. We hope that by the end of the book you will be able to work out how these programs do their job; but to gain confidence early on it's a good idea to try running other people's programs. It also gives you some idea of what the 1000 can be made to do.

The programs are generally accompanied by Program Notes, which explain various oddities, and occasionally suggest modifications to the programs, or projects for you to try in related areas. But they will run, subject to avoiding errors, whether these notes make any sense to you or not. Most of the programs illustrate particular techniques explained in this book, but some use ideas I don't have space to explain properly. In any case, I assume you are reading the Timex *Manual* as well as this one.

There are some (useful) peculiarities in the 1000 keyboard, and I'll briefly mention these since it can be a little frustrating sometimes trying to get the machine to print on the screen what you think you are typing in.

> Translation Manual for ZX80 users:
> Delete = Rubout    Enter = Newline



Typewriter keys generally have two different *shifts,* one for capital letters and one for lower case letters. I own an old portable typewriter built in 1910 that has *three* shifts, to reduce the number of keys and save space. The 1000 has, effectively, *six* shifts, at least on most keys; in other words, a given key can produce up to six different symbols. Most difficulties in getting what you want occur when, by mistake, you press the right key but get the wrong shift.

To understand this, let's take a look at the key with a capital W on it. Over the top of this key you'll see UNPLOT; underneath COS; and on the key itself OR and the graphics character ▙. Here's how you choose which of the six possibilities get printed. (Yes, *six,* see below!)

(1) If you press the key when the machine is at the start of a program line, or when there is only a line number in front of it, or if the preceding character is THEN, the effect will be UNPLOT. The 1000 knows that it is expecting a *keyword*—a command like GOTO, RUN, RETURN, or whatever, telling it to *do* something —and that asking it to "do" W makes no sense. So, clever thing that it is, it knows you want UNPLOT.

(2) Otherwise, assuming you haven't done the things listed below, it will print W.

(3) If you press SHIFT (the only key on the whole keyboard that means only one thing!) with one finger and, still pressing it down, press the W key, you will get OR.

(4) If you put the keyboard into "function" mode—that is, press SHIFT *and* FUNCTION/ENTER at the same time, which gives an [F] cursor—and then remove your fingers before pressing the W (unshifted) you will get COS.

(5) If you put the keyboard into "graphics" mode—by pressing SHIFT and at the same time GRAPHICS/9, which gives a [G]

cursor—and then remove both fingers and then press W, you get [W]—an inverse video W. (The missing member of the six, not shown on the key for pretty obvious reasons . . . )

(6) If you put the keyboard into graphics mode as in (5), but press SHIFT as well as W, you get the graphics character ▛.

The other keys work exactly the same as the W key, and have the possible effects marked on them in the corresponding positions. Number (5) above, inverse video, is not marked on any key, but it is available on all keys except SHIFT and FUNCTION/ENTER. (The inverse video version of SPACE is a black square—yes, *that's* where it is!)

For ZX80 owners Sinclair now has an 8K Extended BASIC plug in unit that comes with a keyboard overlay and the ZX81 *Manual*. This upgrades your ZX80 to have all the key features of the ZX81 (it does not include continuous display) including mathematical and scientific functions accurate to eight decimal places.

DE BUGS

ROMs, RAMs, and REMs . . . Computer jargon isn't really confusing. It just looks like it is.

# Basic BASIC

There is nothing fundamentally mysterious about computers. They're just machines which will carry out series of instructions. Of course the actual *way* they carry them out—now that is truly mysterious, at least if you don't have a degree in solid state physics. But, just as you can drive a car without being able to build one, so you can program a computer without knowing how to design one. *Some* understanding of the actual mechanics of the thing—what computer people call the *hardware*—is useful though, just as it helps to know how a clutch works when you're learning how to change gear, or indeed wondering why it is necessary to change gear at all. But the main principles of programming don't depend much on the hardware, as far as the ordinary user is concerned.

Machines that carry out instructions have been with us for a long time now. Blaise Pascal, a French mathematician-cum-philosopher, built a calculating machine in 1642. Charles Babbage, an Englishman, designed an ambitious "Analytical engine" in 1835, and the British government was persuaded to invest in it. Like other government projects, it turned out not to be feasible with the technology of the time; but the underlying ideas were original and sound. The Frenchman Joseph-Marie Jacquard, at the beginning of the nineteenth century, developed a system using holes punched in cards to control the weave produced by a loom. Fairground steam-organs use a similar principle. Indeed you can think of a trained orchestra as a machine to produce music, with the written sheet music acting as a "program". It's not a bad analogy.



It's no good walking up to a Jacquard loom, saying "seven yards of blue and green check tweed, please," and expecting much useful to happen. It doesn't talk that language. All it understands is a pattern of punched holes; and there are all sorts of restrictions on the size, number, and arrangement of those holes. "Auld Lang Syne" on a steam-organ won't run on a loom—and even if it did, it would produce a result that bore little resemblance to the original tune. You have to know *which* pattern of holes is required to produce the desired pattern of threads in the cloth. So the pattern of holes is a kind of *coded* version of the pattern of threads, with the mechanism of the loom acting as a go-between.

Similarly the written music used by an orchestra is a coded version of the intended musical sounds, with the orchestra itself as an intermediary. (There is a minor difference: orchestras are not as precise as a machine, and a conductor has some freedom to interpret the music. But it's close.)

It is the same with computers, only more so. A given machine must be talked to in a language that it understands.

In the early days of computing, this meant that you would have to type out long lists looking something like this: 0100011101001101011111111000101100010100011 . . . which is kind of hard on the eye. Computers still, "deep down", *think* this way (with "0" meaning "no electrical current" and "1" meaning "some electrical current"): this rather rudimentary language is the *machine code* for the chosen type of computer. Miraculously, it lets you do everything you want to; and it generally has the advantage of being *fast* to run . . . but it's less than straightforward to write programs in it.

Fortunately, these days you don't have to.

This is because a computer can be *taught* to accept commands in a language other than its "native tongue". What actually happens is that some diligent programmer works out a kind of "dictionary" to translate the new language into machine code, and feeds it into the computer (either from some outside source, or built into the hardware). The dictionary is known as a *compiler*, or *interpreter* (depending on just how it works).

The 1000 has a built-in interpreter for a language known as BASIC, which stands for "Beginners' All-purpose Symbolic Instruction Code". This language was developed in the USA in the mid-1960s and is very widely used. It has the advantage of being relatively straightforward, like a cross between ordinary English and school algebra. As far as the beginning programmer is concerned, the 1000 speaks only BASIC. (But the machine language Z80 is accessible via the USR key—and if you don't know *why* you might want to use it, you *don't*. Not yet, anyway.)

## A BASIC PROGRAM

Rather than starting with the "grammar" of BASIC, let's take a look at a simple BASIC program and see what it does and how it does it. The advantage of this is that you'll see right away how easy it is. Grammatical fine points will come later.

```
1∅  PRINT "SQUARE ROOTS"
2∅  INPUT X
3∅  LET Y = SQR X
4∅  PRINT X,Y
5∅  STOP
```

You can probably guess what this does, just by looking at it (HINT: SQR means "square root of"). But first, there are some points to notice about the form that it takes.

(a) It consists of a series of *lines*.
(b) Each line is a "legal" (that is, logically sensible) BASIC *instruction* or *command*, or *statement*. (These three words all mean the same thing in practice.)
(c) Each line starts with a number, known (not surprisingly) as the *line number*. (Computers often use ∅ for zero to distinguish from the letter O.)

To these rather obvious remarks I must add some clarifications. Some of these apply to *all* BASIC interpreters, as used on other machines; some only to the 1000. To save breath I'm not going to worry which is which: if you graduate to a more fancy machine you'll soon find out.

There's nothing worth saying about (a) except that on the 1000 a program line can be more than one line long when written on the TV screen—the machine doesn't mind.

Details for (b) depend on the "grammar" of BASIC, to which we shall come.

The reason for numbering lines (c) is that, early in your programming career, you are going to want to tell the machine to obey specific lines in a program. An instruction "GOTO 73∅" will tell it to do whatever it says on line 73∅ . . . but it needs to know which line that is. There are advantages in *not* just counting "1, 2, 3, . . .", as we shall see. The line number must be a whole number between 1 and 9999 inclusive.

When the machine works its way through a program, it moves from a given line to the next one (except when told to go elsewhere, as part of the program). So it needs those line numbers, even if the programmer himself doesn't want to refer to them. The 1000 will not accept program lines without a number (although it may instead carry out the command for that line, as if it were a pocket calculator). *Don't forget the line numbers!*

## WHAT DOES IT DO?

Type the above program into your 1000. I'm going to assume you know how to do this: if not, reread the previous section and then read pages 21 to 25 of the book *Timex User Manual* that came with it when you bought it.*

Right. So you've got the program typed out, up there on the TV screen, but nothing's happening yet. This is because computers not only obey instructions, but they are fundamentally as thick as two short planks: even when it's obvious what you want them to do, you have to tell them anyway. So press key R (which comes out as RUN) and then ENTER so that it knows you've finished the command.

What you see on the screen is something like RUN [L] where, as you will find throughout this book, boxes denote "inverse video characters"—a white L on a black square. Then this disappears as you hit ENTER.

Across the screen appears the message SQUARE ROOTS. This is the computer's response to line 1∅: PRINT "SQUARE ROOTS". It's done this pretty quickly, and now it's waiting for *you* to do *your* bit of line 2∅: INPUT X. To remind you, there's an [L] at lower left of the screen. It wants you to tell it what X is.

To do this, type out a number, followed by ENTER. Try

25 ENTER



*Hereafter called the *Manual*.

Quick as a flash, the computer types out

25

at the top of the screen. A second or so later it adds to this, giving

25 5

(and, in the lower corner, a message 9/5∅ which we won't worry about—it just means it's finished the job correctly.)

Try it again. To do this, just type RUN followed by ENTER and it's off again. When it asks for X, try something else: if you try 756.2912 and hit ENTER you should get

756.2912 27.5∅∅749

RUN it a few more times, trying different INPUTs X. Try some at random. Try ∅, 1, 4, 9, 16.

This ought to convince you that whatever you input as X, the machine PRINTs out two numbers: first X, and then the square root of X to a fair number of decimal places.

I'm assuming here that you INPUT a sensible X—positive and not too big for the machine. Just for fun, try setting X at −2. You'll get a message in the bottom left, saying A/3∅. This is the computer's way of objecting to being asked to take the square root of a negative number . . . and it refuses to do it.

Experiment. You should get things like

```
49         7
6E + 17    77459667∅
5E + 3∅    2.236∅68E + 15
```

(The E things are numbers in exponential notation; see page 53 of the *Manual*.)

## HOW DOES IT DO IT?

I don't mean in detail—that would get us into the hardware, machine language, and such complexities. But how should you, the programmer, think of the machine, as it runs your program? What's going on inside its tiny silicon-chip brain? Indulging in a little anthropomorphism, it's something like this.

| | |
|---|---|
| 1∅ PRINT "SQUARE ROOTS"<br>2∅ INPUT X<br>3∅ LET Y = SQR X<br>4∅ PRINT X,Y<br>5∅ STOP | Well, gosh, here come some instructions for me to remember. Better do it.<br>I wonder if he's finished yet? |
| RUN ENTER | Yep. Off we go. What's the first line? Get it from memory: 1∅ PRINT "SQUARE ROOTS".<br>I've got to PRINT something.<br>There's a quotation mark "; then I copy out what follows . . . |
| SQUARE ROOTS | until I reach another". Which tells me to stop PRINTing.<br>Nothing else. On to next line: 2∅ INPUT X. He's going to tell me a number, and I've got to call it X. Give him an . . . |
| [L] | cursor to remind him.<br>OK, I'm waiting.<br>Dead slow, these humans. |
| 25 ENTER | Ah. X is 25. Now what? 3∅ LET Y = SQR X. That means I must work out the square root of X . . . which is $\sqrt{25}$, namely 5; and call the result Y. So Y is 5. |

Next instruction? 4∅ PRINT X, Y. I have to PRINT X and Y, which are . . .

25 5

Next line? 5∅ STOP. That's the lot, then. Finish with a report . . .

9/5∅

Ignore the whimsy: do you see how the machine is just running through the list of commands, and obeying them as they come? It doesn't even "know" what the program is about. But you, the programmer, know—it calculates square roots.

The task of the programmer is now clear. Given a job that you want the machine to do, you must assemble a series of instructions which, when carried out, achieve this objective.

To do this, you'll need to know BASIC in more detail. Your 1000 will do some pretty clever things if you know how to talk to it. There are all sorts of refinements, of course—a *good* program should be quick, efficient, and clear, as well as getting the job done. But refinements can wait: the main thing is to write programs that *work*.

So let's get started.

Addition, subtraction, multiplication, and division form the basis of all mathematics. The same goes for computing. So the sensible place to start is by explaining how to do:

# ARITHMETIC IN BASIC

Actually that's a lie—it's algebra. But I didn't want to scare you off. Algebraic calculations are involved in almost any program you care to write, even if only for book-keeping purposes, so they're a reasonable place to start.

Just like ordinary algebra, BASIC uses letters to stand for "general" numbers. In the jargon, these are called *variables*—indeed, *numeric* variables—but really all this means is that they are things like X, Y, Z, A, B, C and so on which can be used to build up algebraic expressions like X + Y − Z, which the computer can then work out if you tell it, via the program, what values X, Y, and Z take. (For instance if X = 14, Y = 3, Z = 9 then X + Y − Z = 14 + 3 − 9 = 8.) On the 1000 you can use more complicated symbols for variables than just single letters; but since these look more like ordinary algebra, it seems better to stick to just single letters at first. Anyway, long names waste memory.

There are some small but important differences between BASIC algebra and ordinary algebra. First, the letters are all in capitals—in fact you can't print lower case. The signs + (plus), − (minus), and / (divided by) are just as usual. (You can't use ÷) But multiplication is written as an asterisk *, so that 5*7 means 5 × 7, which is 35. The double-asterisk symbol ** (shifted H: two copies of *, shifted B, will *not* be correctly interpreted by the computer, so be careful) means "raised to the power". For instance, 2**3 means what an algebraist would write as $2^3$, which is 2 to the power of 3 (or 2 *cubed*) and has value 2 × 2 × 2 = 8.



You can combine numbers, variables, and these arithmetical signs to produce more complicated expressions. For instance

A*X**2 + B*X + C

is the algebraist's favourite $ax^2 + bx + c$.

Chapter 11 of the *Manual* explains about these, and it makes a very important point about the order in which the machine makes the calculations. Suppose, in the above expression, the machine knows that A = 4, X = 5, B = 3, C = 7. You might think that it will work out the sum as follows:

A*X = 4*5 = 2∅,
A*X**2 = 2∅**2 = 4∅∅,
A*X**2 + B = 4∅∅ + B = 4∅3,
A*X**2 + B*X = 4∅3*X = 2∅15,
A*X**2 + B*X + C = 2∅15 + C = 2∅22.

That's what you get if you work along the expression from left to right. But this will not correspond to the algebraist's $ax^2 + bx + c$, which would take the value

$4 \times 5^2 + 3 \times 5 + 7 = 1∅∅ + 15 + 7 = 122.$

So what's gone wrong?*

The point is that ordinary algebra is full of rules, about which operations you do first. (Anyone remember a thing called BODMAS? Never mind . . . ) And the language BASIC has similar rules. In fact it works out all **'s *first,* then all *'s and /'s, and finally the +'s and −'s. If in doubt, it does each of these in order from left to right. So it actually works out A*X**2 + B*X + C this way:

| | |
|---|---|
| First do the **'s: | X**2 = 5*2 = 25 |
| Now the *'s: | A*X**2 = 4*25 = 1∅∅ |
| | B*X = 3*5 = 15. |
| Now the +'s: | A*X**2 + B*X = 1∅∅ + 15 = 115 |
| | A*X**2 + B*X + C = 115 + C = 115 + 7 = 122. |

You can see how this resembles ordinary algebra.

Just as in algebra, you sometimes want to work out an expression which does *not* follow these rules naturally. The solution is the same: you use *brackets* ( ). Any expression inside brackets is worked out as a whole first. So

```
(A*X)**2
```

would be worked out as (4*5)**2, which is (2∅)**2 if you do the bracketed bit first, and this is 4∅∅.

There is only one kind of bracket (not like [ ] or { } in algebra). So you have to be especially careful when putting brackets inside other brackets, writing things like (3 + 5*(A − B))**4 where an algebraist would write $[3 + 5(a - b)]^4$.

The main thing to understand is that it really is just like ordinary algebra with slightly unfamiliar symbols.

## ASSIGNING A VALUE TO A VARIABLE

This is done by the LET statement (key L). If you use it where it ought to be used, the clever 1000 automatically recognizes it as LET and not L (by a process known as "automatic syntax-checking" which just means it keeps an eye on what makes sense as you type it in). A program line such as

```
4∅   LET X = 5
```

tells the computer that the variable X takes the value 5 *from now on, and until it is told otherwise by some other part of the program*. Try this program.

```
1∅   LET A = 4
2∅   LET B = 3
3∅   LET C = 7
4∅   LET X = 5
5∅   PRINT A*X**2 + B*X + C
```

If all is well in that diminutive skull, you will see the answer 122 popping up at the top of the screen.

There are easier ways to get this particular answer: try

```
1∅   PRINT 4*5**2 + 3*5 + 7
```



(You can even omit the line number; see Chapter 4 of the *Manual*, 'Mathematics with the T/S 1000'. But we want you to see how LET works.)

The right-hand side of a LET command can be an expression that the computer already knows how to work out. For instance, you could change line 5∅ of the above program to define a new variable Y, taking the value A*X**2 + B*X + C:

```
5∅   LET Y = A*X**2 + B*X + C
```

Follow this by

```
6∅   PRINT Y
```

and you can check it works properly.

### EXAMPLE: FALLING BODIES

According to Galileo, a body falling from rest under gravity will drop a distance of (approximately) $16t^2$ feet in a time of t seconds. To find out how far it will drop in 17 seconds, you could use the program

```
1∅   LET T = 17
2∅   PRINT 16*T**2
```

You should get 4624(feet) as output.

If you want the answer for a different time, you can change the first line of the program. Try it. How far will the body fall in

(a) 97 seconds?
(b) 3 seconds?
(c) 24.5779 seconds?
(d) 1∅∅∅∅1 seconds?

## AN IMPROVEMENT: THE INPUT STATEMENT

You will probably have got fed up with repeatedly changing that line 1∅. A more civilized program would make use of the INPUT command, which lets the machine ask you what value a variable takes. Type out



```
1∅   INPUT T
2∅   PRINT 16*T**2
```

and RUN it. The [L] cursor comes up: this is the machine waiting to be told what T is. Type in 17, then ENTER; you'll get the answer we had at first. But now, to answer (a) to (d), all you have to do is type RUN again, but tell it the new value of T. Try it.

## PROGRAM PROJECTS

Here are three programs for you to write, using just the commands we've looked at so far. They are minor variations on the program for falling bodies. If you get stuck, there's a crib at the end of this chapter!

(e) The volume of a cube whose side is x is given by $x^3$ (that is, X**3 in BASIC if X denotes the side). Write a program which INPUTs X and PRINTs the volume of the corresponding cube.

(f) A bucket is attached to one end of a rope, which is coiled around a windlass shaped like a cylinder of radius r. For this particular bucket, according to the mechanics textbooks, its downward acceleration is given by

$$a = \frac{32}{1 + 3r^2}$$

Don't worry about the mechanics; but write a program which lets you INPUT r and PRINT the acceleration a.

(g) At the local Supermart, honey costs 61 cents a jar: Zxo cubes 25 cents a packet: Whizxas Supermeat 89 cents a can. Write a program which PRINTs the total cost of H jars of honey, Z packets of Zxo cubes, and W tins of Whizxas Supermeat, when you input H, Z and W. [You will need three INPUT commands.]

## A FORETASTE OF LOOPING

The commands FOR and NEXT allow us to try out some of the previous ideas without doing too much work. (In many circles the avoidance of work is called "laziness", but programmers have an advantage over ordinary mortals—they can call it "efficient programming" and point to savings in computer memory or time to prove it.) There's a lot that can be said about FOR/NEXT loops, and in a few pages we'll say it at suitable length. Run this program first, to see the kind of thing that can be done.

```
1Ø   FOR X = 1 TO 2Ø
2Ø   PRINT X, X*X
3Ø   NEXT X
```

You will find a list of the numbers from 1 to 2Ø, and a corresponding list of their squares 1, 4, 9, . . . 361,4ØØ. What the FOR/NEXT commands do is to send the machine round and round the series of commands in between (here just line 2Ø) setting the variable X successively at 1, 2, 3, . . . until 2Ø is reached. Line 1Ø sets these limits up and starts the loop going: line 3Ø sends the computer through the loop again.

By changing line 2Ø in this little program, you can tabulate all sorts of things. You want cubes? Try

```
2Ø   PRINT X, X**3
```

Change line 2Ø to each of the following, and notice the differences. The very minor changes from one to the next cause the machine to work out the algebra in different orders, with differing results. What are the programs calculating in ordinary algebraic symbolism?

```
(h)  2Ø   PRINT X, 1/X + 1
(i)  2Ø   PRINT X, 1/(X + 1)
(j)  2Ø   PRINT X, 1/1 + X
(k)  2Ø   PRINT X, 1/(1 + X)
(l)  2Ø   PRINT X, 1 + 1/X
(m)  2Ø   PRINT X, (1 + 1)/X
```

Finally, notice that in these programs the values of the variable are not assigned by the command LET. The machine obtains the assignment instead from the FOR command.

## ANSWERS

### FALLING BODIES

(a) 15∅544
(b) 144
(c) 9665.1707
(d) 16∅∅∅32∅∅∅∅∅. Don't be deceived by the apparent precision. The computer won't give 12 significant-digit accuracy. It has rounded off the true answer, which is 16∅∅∅32∅∅∅16.

### PROGRAM PROJECTS

(e)
```
1∅   INPUT X
2∅   PRINT X**3
```
(f)
```
1∅   INPUT R
2∅   PRINT 32/(1 + 3*R**2)
```
(g)
```
1∅   INPUT H
2∅   INPUT Z
3∅   INPUT W
4∅   PRINT 61*H + 25*Z + 89*W
```

Your program doesn't have to look *exactly* like these to be "correct". In particular, the choice of symbols for variables is entirely up to you. You can do the algebra other ways, too; in (e) there's nothing wrong with 2∅ PRINT X*X*X, and in (f) with 2∅ PRINT 32/(1 + 3*R*R).

### LOOPING

(h) $\frac{1}{x} + 1$ (i) $\frac{1}{x + 1}$

(j) 1 + x [it works out 1/1 first, which is 1, then adds on x] (k) the same as (i)

(l) the same as (h) (m) $\frac{2}{x}$

Not going as well as you hoped? Maybe you can use some . . .

# HEEEEELLLLPPPPP!

If something doesn't quite go right, what should you do?

At the very worst, you unplug the power supply for a second. This crashes the program, wipes out everything you've written in—but unjams whatever the trouble was (unless in the hardware, in which case hard luck). But there are usually better ways.

(a) If you print the wrong thing in a program line: Use the arrowed keys 5 and 8 (note you need SHIFT) to move the [L] cursor just past the offending beast, obliterate it using DELETE.

(b) If you want to change a line that's already gone into the program: To delete it altogether, write its line number and press ENTER. Otherwise, move the [>] cursor up and down the lines using 6 and 7: then press EDIT to bring the line down to where it can work on it. Now proceed as in (a).
*Various tricks:* It's an awful pain to move the cursor from line 1∅ to line 53∅ one line at a time. Find a line number just before 53∅ that you haven't used, say 529. Write 529 ENTER; then press EDIT. You'll see line 53∅ come down. (Why?) Or use LIST 53∅, then EDIT. If the screen gets full, you need to press CLS before doing the EDIT.

(c) If the program gets stuck, and nothing seems to be happening: This is often the case during a debugging session: the last thing you want is to wipe everything out and type it all in again; and in any case it's likely to do exactly the same again.

(c1) If the program is still executing, but you want to stop it: Press BREAK

(c2) If it's stuck on a numerical INPUT instruction: BREAK won't work; but STOP will. If by mistake you've got other junk sitting there, it will keep giving you an [S] cursor for a syntax error, which is vastly frustrating; DELETE the junk, then STOP.

(c3) If it's stuck on a character input—"L" cursor: This is the one the *Manual* doesn't mention, and it cost me an hour's work in lost program once. Silly me: press DELETE and *then* STOP.

(d) If the program runs but doesn't do the right things: Read the DEBUGGING articles, below.

(e) If you invent a new way to get stuck, *let me know:* with luck this book will go to a new edition one of these days!

There were 10 in the bed and the little one said
"Roll over, roll over!"
And they all rolled over and one fell out.
There were 9 in the bed and . . .

# LOOPING

By using the FOR and NEXT instructions, you can make the machine carry out an instruction over and over again a specified number of times. This may not sound very interesting, but in fact it is one of the most useful weapons in the programmer's armoury because you can use variables to alter what each step does.

We've already seen how FOR/NEXT loops allow us to print out tables of values of a function like X**3. Here's a slightly less simple use.

The factorial function n! is defined, as every schoolboy knows, to be:

$$n! = n(n - 1)(n - 2)(n - 3) \ldots 3 \times 2 \times 1.$$

It tells you the number of possible ways to arrange n objects in order. For instance, $3! = 3 \times 2 \times 1 = 6$; and the letters abc can be arranged in order 6 ways: abc, acb, bac, bca, cab, cba.

To compute n! we can use loops. The idea is to compute it in stages: $1; 1 \times 2; 1 \times 2 \times 3; 1 \times 2 \times 3 \times 4; \ldots$ and to keep going until the largest number is n. In each case you take the result of the *previous* stage and multiply by the next number up. This is just the set-up needed for a loop. In fact, the sequence of statements

```
1Ø  LET I = 1
2Ø  FOR K = 2 TO N
3Ø  LET.I = I*K
4Ø  NEXT K
```

has just this effect.

What does it do? And how? Line 1Ø just sets up a starting value for the variable I. Line 2Ø tells the machine to carry out succeeding lines over and over again, letting K successively take the values 2, 3, 4, 5, . . . , N. Line 4Ø tells it when it has reached the end of these instructions and should go back to the start of the loop again. So the first time through, it takes K = 2, and line 3Ø works out

I = I*K = 1 × 2.

Next time through, K has become 3 and I has become 1 × 2; so it works out I*K which is now 1 × 2 × 3. Next time, K is 4, and it works out 1 × 2 × 3 × 4. And so on, until the final stage, when K is N and it works out I = 1 × 2 × 3 × 4 × . . . × N. Then, thanks to the limits set in line 2Ø, it knows that the loop is finished.

This won't quite work out N! for you, because the program doesn't include instructions for what N is, or to print the answer. So you need to embed the loop in a larger program:

```
5    INPUT N
1Ø   LET I = 1
2Ø   FOR K = 2 TO N
3Ø   LET I = I*K
4Ø   NEXT K
5Ø   PRINT "FACTORIAL □"; N; "□ IS □"; I
```

(Line 5Ø is just fancy printing: you get outputs like

FACTORIAL 6 IS 72Ø.

Notice the spaces, shown as boxes □, to make it look pretty.)

## RABBITTING ON

In about 1220 a gentleman called Leonardo of Pisa, nicknamed Fibonacci (Son of Good Humour) came up with an interesting problem about rabbits.



If a breeding pair of rabbits produces one new pair of offspring once a month, and it takes one month for the new pairs to become productive, and you start with one pair—how does the population grow? (For simplicity we assume exactly regular production each month, and that every pair consists of one male and one female.)

It helps to make a table:

<table>
<tr><th>Month No.</th><th>No. of breeding pairs</th><th>No. of new pairs</th></tr>
<tr><td colspan="3">In Month ∅ we have 1 breeding pair, ∅ new pairs, so we get an entry</td></tr>
<tr><td>∅</td><td>1</td><td>∅</td></tr>
<tr><td colspan="3">In Month 1 we get 1 new pair only:</td></tr>
<tr><td>1</td><td>1</td><td>1</td></tr>
<tr><td colspan="3">In Month 2 we get 1 new pair, and the previous new pair becomes productive:</td></tr>
<tr><td>2</td><td>2</td><td>1</td></tr>
<tr><td colspan="3">In Month 3 all of these are productive, and we get 2 new pairs</td></tr>
<tr><td>3</td><td>3</td><td>2</td></tr>
<tr><td colspan="3">and so on:</td></tr>
<tr><td>4</td><td>5</td><td>3</td></tr>
<tr><td>5</td><td>8</td><td>5</td></tr>
<tr><td>6</td><td>13</td><td>8</td></tr>
<tr><td>7</td><td>21</td><td>13</td></tr>
</table>

We're starting to get an awful lot of rabbits, which isn't really surprising.

If we let the total number of pairs of rabbits in Month M be F(M), then we have F(∅) = 1, F(1) = 2, F(2) = 3, F(3) = 5, F(4) = 8, and so on.

Now let's think more generally. Suppose in Month M we have B breeding pairs and N new pairs. Then next month all of these become productive, giving B + N *breeding* pairs; and the B breeders give us B *new* pairs. So the table has two consecutive lines looking like this:

| Month No. | No. of breeding pairs | No. of new pairs |
|---|---|---|
| M | B | N |
| M+1 | B+N | B |

This table suggests how we can calculate F(M) by using loops. The idea is that to get from month M to month M + 1 we have to turn the old B into B + N, and the old N into B. This will work:

```
1∅   LET B = 1
2∅   LET N = ∅
3∅   INPUT M
4∅   FOR T = 1 TO M
5∅   LET C = B
6∅   LET B = B + N
7∅   LET N = C
8∅   NEXT T
9∅   PRINT "F(";M;") □ IS □"; B + N
```

If you study this you'll see that it follows exactly the steps used to build up the table. Lines 1∅ and 2∅ set the initial values of B and N. Line 3∅ asks what value of M we want F(M) for. Lines 4∅ to 8∅ perform a loop which generates successive lines of the table. Note line 5∅, which remembers the *old* B value, calling it C, for use in line 7∅. (If you didn't do this, line 6∅ would change B too soon, and line 7∅ would produce the wrong N value.)

The numbers F(M) are called *Fibonacci numbers*. If you notice that the B and N columns in the table contain the same numbers, but shifted one line apart (why?) you'll see that F(M + 2) = F(M + 1) + F(M); that is, any Fibonacci number is the sum of the previous two.

What is the value of F(14)? F(77)?

## NESTED LOOPS

Even better—you can put loops-within-loops, or even loops-within-loops-within- . . . -loops (as far as the memory can hold). You'd be surprised how often this is necessary.

For instance, suppose you want to print out a table of values of the factorial function. You can use a loop like the one for X**3 on page 15; but then you need *another* loop for the n! calculation. So you get something like this:

```
 5   FOR N = 1 TO 2∅          ┐
1∅   LET I = 1                │
2∅   FOR K = 2 TO N   ┐       │
3∅   LET I = I*K      │ inner loop │ outer loop
4∅   NEXT K           ┘       │
5∅   PRINT N, I               │
6∅   NEXT N                   ┘
```

Notice that the "FOR N/ NEXT N" loop is completely outside the "FOR K/ NEXT K" one. You have to do this to make sense —it's just like brackets. An expression [a + (b − 2c)] + d makes good sense; but [a + (b − 2c]) + d does not. Try interchanging lines 4∅ and 6∅ and see what happens. Not much use, is it? The trouble is, the 1000 will accept, and run, programs with wrongly nested loops; but of course the results are not what you intend. It does *not* print out an error message. Be careful!

## STEP SIZE

If you just write FOR I = 1 TO 2∅ the machine *assumes* you want the variable I to take values 1, 2, 3, 4, 5, . . . , 19, 2∅. That is, it assumes you move up in *steps* of size 1.

But you don't have to do this. You can set a different step size using the key STEP. For example, the instruction

```
1∅   FOR J = −3 TO 3 STEP .5
```

makes J run through the value −3, −2.5, −2, −1.5, −1, −∅.5, ∅, ∅.5, 1, 1.5, 2, 2.5, 3. Similarly,

```
1∅   FOR J = 3 TO 4 STEP .∅1
```

runs through the values 3, 3.∅1, 3.∅2, 3.∅3, . . . going up in hundredths until it ends with 3.98, 3.99, 4.

You can also STEP downwards:

```
1∅   FOR J = 1∅ TO ∅ STEP −1
```

makes J run through the sequence 1∅, 9, 8, 7, 6, 5, 4, 3, 2, 1, ∅. Reminds you of something? Run this program.

```
1∅   FOR J = 1∅ TO ∅ STEP −1
2∅   PRINT J
3∅   NEXT J
4∅   PRINT "BLAST-OFF"
```

Hardly sophisticated, but . . .

There's a little bit of unpredictability built into the 1000.

# RANDOM NUMBERS

The instruction RND produces a "random" number between ∅ and 1, which can equal ∅ but not 1. Actually it's not really random, it's a *pseudo*random number, and the numbers repeat every 65537 times, but you won't notice this in practice. Since nobody knows what a "random" number really looks like, the use of "pseudo" is a bit pseudo itself.

You can use this in game programs. For instance, to simulate the throw of a die, you note that 6*RND is a random number between ∅ and 6 (not including 6), so INT(6*RND) is either ∅,1,2, 3,4 or 5, at random; so 1 + INT(6*RND) is one of 1,2,3,4,5,6 at random. Which is what a die does. (Die is the singular of "dice".) To pick a random card from a pack of 52 you'd play a similar game using 52*RND, but you'd need a fancy bit of programming to convert numbers between ∅ and 51 into names of cards like "JACK OF CLUBS". It can be done if you're cunning.

You can also use random numbers to do statistical simulations. There's a nice example of this on page 131, MONOPOLY DICE.

It is said that the colorful term "getting the bugs out" arose in the early days of computing, when insects used to crawl inside the machine and cause short circuits. Nowadays, if the computer goes wrong, it's usually the programmer's fault. But to put it right, you still need to know about . . .

# DEBUGGING I

It is a hard fact of life, which all programmers learn very rapidly, that programs hardly ever work—at least, the first time they run. The process of eliminating the errors from a program is known as *debugging*. It is important to adopt a systematic approach to this process because, even in a fairly small program, the source of error is not necessarily easy to find. And there are few things more frustrating than programs with elusive bugs in them.

Let's look first at the kinds of error that can occur. Broadly, they split into two groups: *syntax error* and *runtime error*.

## SYNTAX ERRORS

These are errors which the machine can identify as soon as you have typed them in. For example, suppose I were to type the line

```
5Ø   FOR P = 1 - 7
```

under the misapprehension that the "−" symbol can be used as a synonym for "TO". (This is, if you like, an error in the use of the grammar of the language, hence the term "syntax".)

The 1000 is particularly helpful to the beginner in this case. It will allow you to type the "−" symbol; but it will realize that there are no circumstances in which a complete program line can appear as 5Ø FOR P = 1 − 7, and it will display an [S] prompt symbol (to tell you there is a syntax error), and refuse to accept the line until the offending "−" is replaced. (Many popular microcomputers will be perfectly happy to allow you to sprinkle misstatements like this one throughout a program, and will only object when you try to run it. This doesn't matter to an experienced programmer, but the beginner tends to make many such errors, and it saves a lot of time to be told of them immediately.)

At this point a question may be worrying some readers, which we could phrase thus: "If the 1000 knows that the only thing which can appear after the '1' in statement 5∅ is the keyword 'TO', why doesn't the machine insert 'TO' of its own accord?"

The answer is that it doesn't quite know enough to do this. For instance, another digit could follow the "1", as in

```
5∅   FOR P = 12 TO 4∅
```

(There are other, more complicated possibilities. The command

```
5∅   FOR P = 1 - 7 TO 5
```

is legal, and means the same as 5∅ FOR P = −6 TO 5.)

The [S] prompt can appear before you reach the end of a line. For example,

```
2∅   LET E*S = Q
```

The machine expects to find an "=" symbol—or another letter or number—after E, so it can issue the [S] prompt in front of the "*"; although it does not do this until after "enter" is hit.

So the rule with syntax errors is: *watch for the* [S] *prompt.* When it appears the reason will usually be fairly obvious. If it isn't, check the statement you are writing against the appropriate sections of the *Manual.* (One source of error that is occasionally perplexing occurs if you accidentally type out a keyword in full, rather than using its special key. For instance, if you type the two letters "T" and "O" instead of the keyword "TO". The machine will not accept this, although there is no difference on the screen.)

## RUNTIME ERRORS

There are many different types of error that can occur when a program is run. I once came across a computer routine that would only work for programs with an even number of characters, because of a rather subtle error; before it was fixed, you could get round it by adding an extra character, somewhere harmless, to anything that failed to run!

It is more useful to give specific examples of possible errors than to define them in general terms. To begin with, consider the following piece of code:

```
1∅   FOR P = −5 TO 5
2∅   LET A = 1∅/P
3∅   PRINT A
4∅   NEXT P
```

Each of the lines is perfectly valid BASIC and so no syntax errors would be indicated. In fact the program will begin to execute perfectly after "RUN" is entered, and will output

```
−2          [i.e. 1∅/(−5)]
−2.5        [i.e. 1∅/(−4)]
−3.3333333  [i.e. 1∅/(−3)]
−5          [i.e. 1∅/(−2)]
−1∅         [i.e. 1∅/(−1)]
```

But it will then halt with the error message

```
6/2∅
```

Here the problem is pretty clear—even without looking up the error number in the *Manual*. First, the message shows that the machine is objecting to line 2∅, which reads

```
2∅   LET A = 1∅/P
```

Second, this statement has already been executed several times without any fuss; so the problem must be with one of the quantities which is *changing,* that is, the value of A or P. The value of P which has just been successfully dealt with is −1, so the current value of P is ∅. In other words, the machine is trying to work out 1∅/∅, which is infinite (or not defined according to taste) and so cannot be handled, however large a space the machine allocates for the answer.



You probably reached this conclusion long before completing the (rather laborious) analysis above; but I'm using this simple example to illustrate the *kinds* of pointers you should look for when an error has you foxed.

(1) Identify the problem line (the number after "/" in the terminating message).
(2) Determine whether this statement has been executed at least once, before generating the error message. (If it has, the problem is with the particular value of one of the variables at the instant when the error occurred.)
(3) Use the report code (*Manual,* p. 153)—the value before "/" in the terminating message—to get a further clue. In the example, this is "6"—and the Timex *Manual* tells you this means "Arithmetic Overflow: calculations have led to a number greater than about $1\varnothing^{38}$." Note that the error message does not say *exactly* what has happened (i.e. it does not say "Attempt to divide by zero"), so it is not always enough simply to look at the error message in the hope that this will explain precisely what has gone wrong.

The problem of dividing by zero crops up fairly often, and not necessarily in such an obvious way as that just described. For instance:

```
1Ø  INPUT P
2Ø  INPUT Q
3Ø  INPUT R
4Ø  LET A = (P + Q − R*2)/(5 + (P − R)*(P − R)−2*Q)
```

will cause the same problem if the values 7, 15, and 2 are entered for P, Q, and R respectively. (Try it!) In general, it makes good sense to test divisors to see if they are zero, before attempting the sum. We might rewrite the above example as follows:

```
 1Ø  INPUT P
 2Ø  INPUT Q
 3Ø  INPUT R
 32  LET D − 5 + (P − R)*(P − R)−2*Q
 34  IF D = Ø THEN GOTO 1ØØ
 4Ø  LET A = (P + Q − R*2)/D
. . .
1ØØ  PRINT "CAN'T DO THIS"
. . .
```



The meaning of the GOTO instruction is (I hope) obvious!

## DEBUGGING PROBLEM

Finally, here's a chance to test your grasp of what has been said so far. The following program is intended to accept a series of positive numbers, and to print out their average. If we wanted to take the average of 2.4, 8.1, 7, and 14 we would enter:

```
 2.4
 8.1
 7
14
-1
```

The "−1" at the end is used solely to indicate that no more data are to be entered, and is *not* part of the data. (Such a value is often called a *delimiter;* and you'll see how it works if you look at line 4Ø of the program below.)

```
 1Ø   LET S = Ø
 2Ø   LET C = Ø
 3Ø   INPUT N
 4Ø   IF N < Ø THEN GOTO 1ØØ
 5Ø   LET C = C + I
 6Ø   LET Z = S + N
 7Ø   GOTO 3Ø
1ØØ   PRINT "AVERAGE IS □"; S/C
```

There are some typographical errors in the listing. See if you can correct them by *entering the program as it stands and tinkering with it*. When you've had a go at it, compare your solution to mine by looking at page 54.

Happy debugging!

# PLOTTING

Not only can the 1000 calculate—it can draw diagrams, too. Not, perhaps, to the standards of Leonardo da Vinci; but certainly well enough to produce attractive displays which illustrate basic principles of computer graphics. The 1000 graphics are "low-resolution"—that is, *coarse*—but all that means is that it plots with big dots in a small space rather than small dots in a large space. So what you can learn using coarse graphics is more widely applicable, given more sophisticated hardware.

In fact the 1000 has two different ways of drawing things: PLOT and PRINT. We'll start by looking at PLOT, which is a bit simpler; PRINT is discussed later, on page 61.

The TV screen, for PLOT purposes, is thought of as being divided up into 2816 tiny squares (actually rectangles) known in the trade as *pixels* (derived from picture elements, but with Americanized spelling). These are labelled by two *coordinates* which tell you how far across the screen from left to right, and how far up, they are. Here's the complete diagram of all 2816 squares. The horizontal coordinate ranges from ∅ to 63; the vertical one from ∅ to 43.

The instruction PLOT X, Y just blacks in the square with horizontal coordinate X and vertical coordinate Y. That's all it does. But that's all you need to draw things: a pencil (blacked in squares), paper (the 64 × 44 array of pixels on the screen), and a way of deciding where to move the pencil to (X and Y).

Similarly, UNPLOT X, Y removes the dot plotted at X, Y (if there is one)—like an eraser.

We have to *build* all the other shapes we might like to display from these two instructions. Suppose we want to plot a horizon-

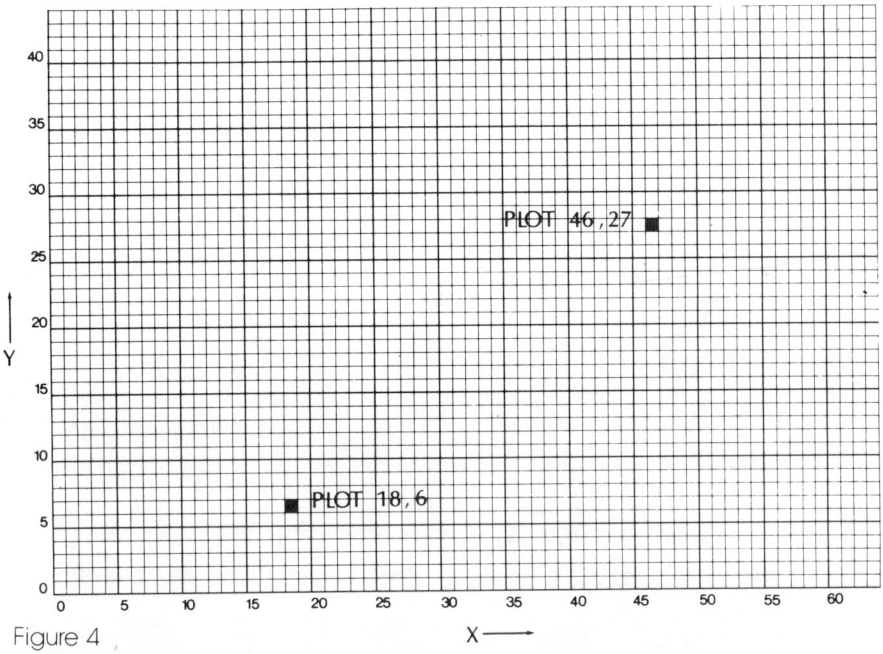


Figure 4

tal line. We can visualize this as a sequence of PLOTted squares side by side. We could write a piece of code like

```
1Ø   PLOT 1Ø,1Ø
2Ø   PLOT 11,1Ø
3Ø   PLOT 12,1Ø
4Ø   PLOT 13,1Ø
5Ø   PLOT 14,1Ø
```

to get a line 5 pixels long at Y = 1Ø.

Since the X value is varying in consistent steps of 1(1Ø,11,12, 13,etc.) there is a good case for rewriting this using a FOR loop:

```
1Ø   FOR X = 1Ø TO 14
2Ø   PLOT X, 1Ø
3Ø   NEXT X
```

It's now easy to build a rectangle, for example. Let's assume that the bottom left corner is defined by the X and Y values LX (<u>L</u>eftmost <u>X</u>) and BY (<u>B</u>ottom <u>Y</u>), and that the height and width are H and W respectively.

The code looks like this:

```
 8Ø   FOR X = LX TO LX + W              ┐
 9Ø   PLOT X,BY                         ├─ plots the bottom edge
1ØØ   NEXT X                            ┘
11Ø   FOR Y = BY TO BY + H              ┐
12Ø   PLOT LX + W,Y                     ├─ plots right-hand side
13Ø   NEXT Y                            ┘
14Ø   FOR X = LX + W TO LX STEP − 1     ┐
15Ø   PLOT X,BY + H                     ├─ plots the top edge
16Ø   NEXT X                            ┘
17Ø   FOR Y = BY + H TO BY STEP − 1     ┐
18Ø   PLOT LX,Y                         ├─ plots left-hand side
19Ø   NEXT Y                            ┘
```

Let's extend this idea. If we can see a line as a collection of pixels, why not see a block as a collection of lines? So something like

```
5ØØ   FOR Y = 2Ø TO 3Ø
51Ø         ┐
52Ø         ├─ plots a line between X = 1Ø and 18
53Ø         ┘
54Ø   NEXT Y
```

should plot a block between Y = 2Ø and 3Ø, and X = 1Ø and 18.

Well, we know what the "plot a line" looks like for any value of Y:

```
FOR X = 1Ø TO 18
PLOT X,Y
NEXT X
```

So the whole thing is:

```
5ØØ   FOR Y = 2Ø TO 3Ø
51Ø   FOR X = 1Ø TO 18
52Ø   PLOT X,Y
53Ø   NEXT X
54Ø   NEXT Y
```

I've labored the development of this construction rather, because the idea of a loop inside another loop is a little confusing to begin with; and although we've met it briefly before, it is not immediately obvious that this is what you need to draw blocks. It is a legitimate and very common construction. (I repeat that each inner loop must be *totally* enclosed within the outer one. It's not a good idea to write

```
 5Ø   FOR X = 2Ø TO 4Ø
 6Ø   FOR Y = 3Ø TO 35
      . . .
1ØØ   NEXT X
11Ø   NEXT Y
```

If you think about it, it doesn't make sense anyway. Curiously, the 1000 will still "obey" it, but the results won't be what you'd expect of a loop within a loop.)

It would be very easy to link the two routines we've got in such a way that we can draw rectangles and blocks all over the screen in any pattern we fancy—a very elementary example of Computer-Aided Design. All we have to do is input the details of the size and shape, check to see if it can fit on the screen (to avoid crashing), ask whether a block or rectangle is to be plotted, and then branch to the appropriate routine. At the end of the routine, go back to the input statements, so that another shape can be entered. The whole thing looks like:

```
 1Ø   INPUT LX
 2Ø   INPUT BY
 3Ø   INPUT H
 4Ø   INPUT W
 45   IF LX + W < = 63 AND BY + H < = 43 THEN GOT TO 6Ø
 5Ø   PRINT AT Ø,Ø;"OFF EDGE"
 55   GO TO 1Ø
 6Ø   INPUT T    (T = Ø for rectangle, 1 for block)
 7Ø   IF T = 1 THEN GO TO 5ØØ
 8Ø   FOR X = LX TO LX + W
 9Ø   PLOT X,BY
1ØØ   NEXT X
11Ø   FOR Y = BY TO BY + H
12Ø   PLOT LX + W,Y
```

```
13∅ NEXT Y
14∅ FOR X = LX + W TO LX STEP - 1
15∅ PLOT X,BY + H
16∅ NEXT X
17∅ FOR Y = BY + H TO BY STEP -1
18∅ PLOT LX,Y
19∅ NEXT Y
2∅∅ GO TO 1∅
5∅∅ FOR Y = BY TO BY + H
51∅ FOR X = LX TO LX + W
52∅ PLOT X,Y
53∅ NEXT X
54∅ NEXT Y
55∅ GO TO 1∅
```

Try the program out, and you'll see we have a simple basis for a graphic design program (provided you like black and white wall-paper). You can probably think of other standard shapes which could be built in (triangles? parallelograms?) as extra routines.

Good programs are worth keeping. On the 1000 you can do this using an ordinary cassette recorder. But there is a definite knack to

# GETTING IT TAPED

You've been working for three hours on a fiendishly complicated program to get Luke Skywalker safely out of the Deathstar, or to calculate the flow of a compressible fluid around a banana, or whatever; and at last it's working. Of course it doesn't take as long to type out the program as it did to get it running in the first place, but it would be a depressing task if you had to do this for every program that you want to keep.

But, thanks to the genius who invented the cassette recorder, you don't have to. You can SAVE programs on tape; and LOAD them into the 1000 as you need them.

If all goes well—and it probably will—there's enough in the *Manual* for you to do the job. But it isn't entirely straightforward, and there are one or two dodges that the *Manual* doesn't mention. I thought you might find them useful.

## SAVEing

You'll need: the 1000, a TV, the usual connecting leads, and of course a cassette recorder. Most makes will work; the cheaper mono ones are *better;* and you very likely have one already and naturally will want to use it if at all possible.

There is a connecting lead for tape with the 1000: two shortish wire leads strapped together, with little black jackplugs at both ends. There's a yellow band at both ends of one lead.

Write a program, on the machine, as usual. It doesn't have to *do* anything, for a test: what you need is a longish list of characters to give yourself time to see what's going on. The quickest way is to use lots of REM statements, followed by junk:

```
1∅   REM "TEST3"
2∅   REM HHHHHHQQQ
etc.
```

as in Figure 5.

Plug the cassette player in and check it's working. (Or run it off batteries, of course—there may even be advantages in this; see later.) Insert a blank cassette or one you don't mind wiping out.

Connect the cassette player MIC socket to the 1000 MIC socket. *At this stage do not connect anything to the EAR or MONITOR sockets.* Use *one* of the two leads Sinclair provide—say, the one with the yellow bands on it. Ignore the other one. (You don't need to pull them apart, though!)

Set the cassette recorder volume to FULL and the tone control to give maximum treble (make it sound as tinny as possible). On most machines this matters little when recording, but you'll need to set them later so you may as well take the precaution now.

Waggle the jackplugs in their sockets to see if they're seating well. You can usually feel if they're "right".

Set the cassette just as you would to make a recording—that is, push the RECORD button and the PLAY button. The tape will start to turn; don't worry, that's what's supposed to happen. There's no great rush. Make sure the cassette has run past the leader tape before the next step.

Press SAVE on the 1000 (that is, key S: it is automatically read as "SAVE") then "" (this is crucial and it won't accept

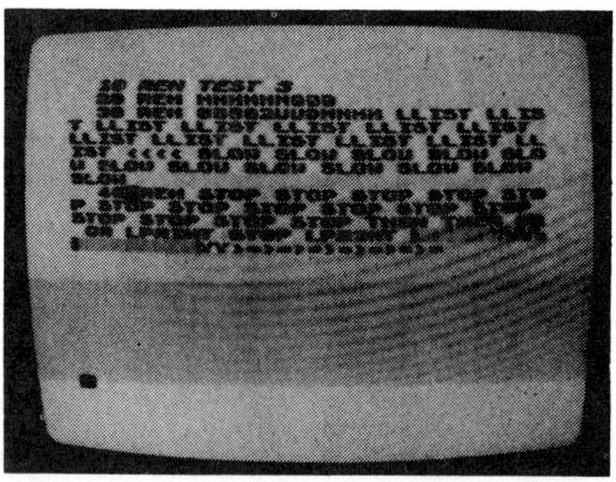

Figure 5 REMs and junk make for quick tests

Figure 6 The program is SAVEing

less) and then ENTER. Things should start to happen on the TV screen.

First, it will go blank for about 5 seconds.

Then you should see a lot of horizontal stripes, as in Figure 6. These are the program going in, and they will stay on the screen for about 15–20 seconds.

Then the screen should clear, with a signal ∅/∅. This means it's finished and it's happy with the result. Stop the recorder.

## HAS IT SAVED?

The trouble is, the ∅/∅ just means the 1000 is happy with what it thinks it sent out; it tells you nothing about what the cassette player picked up. (Try doing it all without a cassette player: the 1000 doesn't notice it's not there.)

To see if the program has been SAVEd properly, you have to try to LOAD it; but before doing that you can check to some extent to see if there is any hope, by listening to the tape.

Just rewind to the starting-point, and PLAY it.

First comes a rather mechanical sort of buzzing sound. This is what the 1000 puts out when it's not actually SAVEing. Sinclair describe it as "soft" but that's not entirely accurate.

Then comes a period of relative silence, corresponding to the screen of the TV going blank. If it *doesn't* sound silent, you may have troubles with things like mains hum; see later.

Then you get a harsh, irregular noise, like high-speed Morse code. This is the program, and corresponds to Figure 6 on the screen. At full volume this will be earsplittingly loud, and you'll need to turn the volume down. (If it's not, you may again have problems.)

## LOADing

So far, all we've done is rehash the *Manual* with added photos; but now you'll get something extra. Let's assume all seems well so far. Now, you'll want to load the program back into the machine.

To convince yourself that what eventually appears really does come from the tape, press NEW and get rid of the program in the 1000. (Now you see why I said to use REMs plus junk: if it doesn't LOAD, you've lost the lot.)

Rewind the tape again.

Disconnect the wire lead between the cassette player and the 1000, and reconnect the EAR socket of the 1000 to the EARphone or MONITOR socket on the cassette player.

Set the volume control on the cassette player to about three-quarters of full. (This is a preliminary guess; you may have to experiment; see later.)

Type LOAD "" on the 1000, followed by ENTER. The screen will change to a pattern like Figure 7, probably without the vertical zigzag.

Start the player running. (Don't hit RECORD by mistake or you'll wipe everything and have to start again.) The screen picture may become a bit erratic for a few seconds, if there are ex-

Figure 7 'Silent' pattern when LOADing

Figure 8 The program is LOADing properly

traneous noises on the tape. When you get to the "silent" bit you should see Figure 7 (or something like it) again.

When the tape reaches the "program" part—Figure 6, going in—everything changes dramatically. You should see something like Figure 8. You may even hear faint Morse code on the TV (vision-on-sound).

As this ends, the screen should clear, with the message Ø/Ø. If so, all is well: type LIST and your program should appear; type RUN and it should work. (Not that REMs *do* much . . .)

But sometimes, it doesn't happen that way—especially first time round. . . .

## IF NOT . . .

Don't despair. At the very worst, Sinclair will send you another one and you'll have $99 tied up for a bit; or you *might* need to fork out $30 or so for a compatible cassette recorder. Probably, it's not that bad.

The picture on the screen give a lot of clues.

(a) It always looks like Figure 7.
First, try repeating the whole thing, but at a higher volume on the player. During the "program" part—Morse code—you may get Figure 7 if the volume is too low. Set it all up as before, but waggle the volume up and down during this section of tape: you'll probably see the screen suddenly changing to Figure 8. The best

. . . like high-speed Morse code . . .

volume is the *lowest* that will reliably produce Figure 8. (This minimizes any danger of hum obliterating the "silent" part.)
Sometimes, this makes no difference. It happened to me, and it took a while to find out what was wrong. The point is that, provided your cassette player gives a good signal in an earphone, the TV screen ought to react with more than just Figure 7; and if it doesn't, there is something wrong with the 1000 or (more likely) the connecting leads.
The jackplugs may not fit well. Wiggle them while trying to LOAD. Wiggle the volume control at the same time.
Test the wire leads for continuity and the absence of short-circuits. (This is what happened to me—there was a short in one of the jackplugs.) An easy way is to use a battery and a flashlight bulb, as shown in the box on page 53.
If neither of these works, send it back to the company. Tell them what make of recorder you've got. Wait. (Sorry, but that's how it is when the hardware goes kaput.)

(b) Instead of Figure 8 you get Figure 9.
Try *lowering* the volume during LOAD. It's probably too high.

(c) It all looks right, but the program still doesn't LOAD, and you don't get ∅/∅.
Most likely culprit is hum on the tape. Battery operation should stop this. (This is why I suggest you don't connect *both* leads: as the *Manual* says, this may set up a feedback loop and cause noise on the tape. In my experience this is quite common.)
If this still won't work, listen to the "silent" bit of tape again. How "silent" is it? If it's noisy, or if the "program" part is a bit fuzzy, you may have a duff recorder.

(d) If still in trouble, try borrowing a friend's cassette recorder, pref-

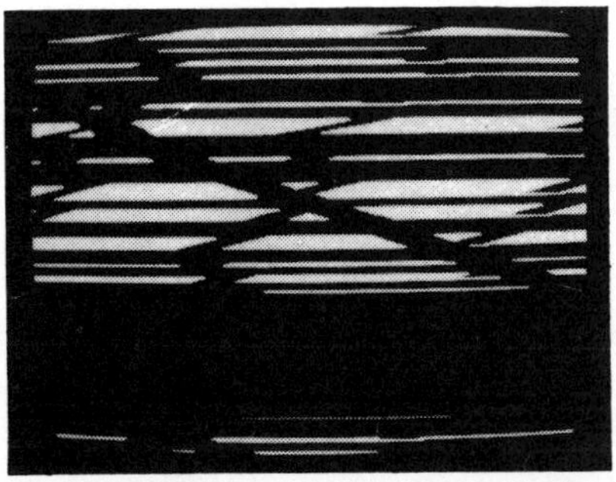

Figure 9 Problems. Try lowering the volume

erably of a different make. Better still, find someone whose 1000 LOADs OK and substitute yours in his set-up to see what's at fault. Contact your local Usergroup if you don't know anyone (see page 121).

## FANCY STUFF

You can *name* a program when you SAVE it, by typing not just

```
SAVE ""
```

but

```
SAVE "MAGGIE"
```

(say.) The 1000 will then know that "MAGGIE" is the program you've just SAVEd. To LOAD it, type

```
LOAD "MAGGIE"
```

and it will ignore all others until MAGGIE shows up. The screen will display all the right pictures for other programs, but not give you the Ø/Ø.

You can test this by running several programs on the tape. The first program line can be used as a reminder of the name use:

```
1Ø  REM "MAGGIE"
```

NB: the LOAD routine does *not* look for this name; it looks for the one used when you SAVEd the program. You can SAVE as

MAGGIE, REM as TONY—and it will still be MAGGIE that has to be LOADed.

## TAPE TIPS

Any reasonable quality tape should work, but the better ones tend to give less noise and better treble response. Use a *short* one (a C30 or C45 if you can get them). There are two reasons for this. (1) You don't want to wait ten minutes for the tape to wind on to the program you're looking for. (2) Short tapes are generally thicker, and you don't get so much "print-through" of magnetic signals with long-term storage.

Record the name of the program just before it on the tape, by speaking into the microphone. This is purely to help you find it again.

If your cassette player has a counter, you're laughing. If not, is it worth the expense of buying another? Think about it.

Keep the cassette heads well cleaned. Cotton swabs and alcohol are best. The 1000 will object to things that sound OK on Barbra Streisand or Siouxsie and the Banshees. Keep the heads demagnetized too.

Use short names—long ones waste typing time on LOAD.

Use "normal bias" tapes unless your cassette recorder has a bias control. (Most don't.)

Even if you've got the volume level worked out for your own SAVEd tapes, you may have to vary it on commercial software tapes because these can be recorded at different levels of volume.

## INCOMPATIBLE CASSETTE PLAYERS

Unless yours is pretty old, or unusual, it shouldn't cause too much trouble. However, problems have sometimes been encountered with the following models:



BOOTS CTR 600; HITACHI TRQ-299; ITT KB SL52; KASUGA KC-8078; PRINTZSOUND TR255C; RT-VC KIT.

These don't *always* give trouble: I used a HITACHI and it worked perfectly, though it was a little sensitive to the volume on LOAD. But if you're experiencing difficulties and you've got one of these, it's wise to try to borrow a different machine to see what happens, *before* sending everything back to the manufacturer (which can take *ages*).

## CONTINUITY-TESTING

Wire up a battery to a flashlight bulb (1.5 volts) with two long ends of wire, as shown. If these ends are touched to a lead that has no breaks, the bulb should light. If they are touched to parts that should be disconnected, the bulb should not light. (If you have a multi-meter, fine; but you shouldn't need to read this bit anyway.)

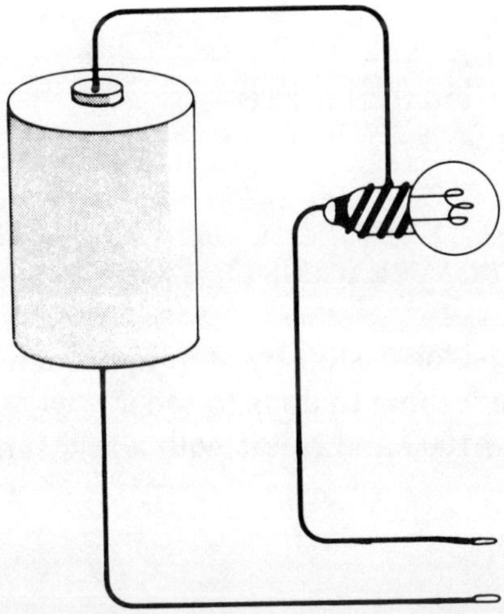

Figure 10

# DEBUGGING II

Earlier I left you with the averaging program which is reproduced below (so you don't have to page-flick too much) and suggested you might like to try debugging it.

```
 1∅   LET S = ∅
 2∅   LET C = ∅
 3∅   INPUT N
 4∅   IF N < ∅ THEN GO TO 1∅∅
 5∅   LET C = C + I
 6∅   LET Z = S + N
 7∅   GO TO 3∅
1∅∅   PRINT "AVERAGE IS □";S/C
```

Let's now consider a step-by-step approach to the problem. Obviously, the first thing to do is to see if it works as it stands, so we key it into the 1000 and run it with a few simple sets of data. Suppose we try:

3
7
5
−1 (remember—this value just acts as a terminator or delimiter)

the answer to which *should* be 5. In fact, when the program is run, you get the error report 2/5∅. Hmmm. It means that a previously undefined variable has been used in line 5∅. From the listing we can see that this is I. So let's give I a value, say



```
5   LET I = ∅
```

That will fix things up so that the program continues beyond line 5∅. If we add line 5 and RUN again, we find that the message

AVERAGE IS

is printed correctly, but then an error report:

6/1∅∅

is displayed.

We've met this message before: you probably remember that the "6" indicates that the machine has attempted to do a piece of arithmetic leading to a result larger than it can hold, and that the "1∅∅" indicates the line number when the problem arose. So a fair bet would be that the program has tried to divide by zero, as was the case the last time this error report cropped up. Before we start the real detective work, let's collect a little more evidence. Try a different set of data:

2
1
4
6
−1

Exactly the same set of messages results. So a working hypothesis seems to be: "Whatever data are entered, the program terminates with an arithmetic overflow report." Test the program with three or four more sets of data and our working hypothesis looks more and more sound.

So, where to start looking? I used the words "detective" and "evidence" a minute ago; I didn't use them lightly. Debugging programs is like detective work, and any detective will tell you that you have to try to think like the villains to be successful, or, if you like, "it takes a thief to catch a thief". The villain of this piece is the 1000, so our problem is to try to think like it. The first thing to do is to slow down your thought processes. That surprised you, didn't it? You were under the impression that computers were a bit quick. Well, so they are, but the way they "think" about a problem is usually pretty laborious. Next, set up a model of the computer's memory, or at least that part of it which is relevant to the problem in hand. In our example, five memory elements have been set up, and have been given the names S, C, N, I and Z. A convenient model, then, will just be a table in which we can show how the contents of these elements change as the program is executed. It can also be helpful to have an indication of the line number at which a branch takes place, although this is not essential. So the table might appear as:

| Line No. | S | C | N | I | Z | Branch |
|---|---|---|---|---|---|---|
| | | | | | | |

I have added an extra column labelled "Branch" whose function I'll deal with shortly. Now we build up the table by considering the action of each statement in turn. We have to define a data set to deal with; let's choose:

2
1
4
6
−1

So, the first statements to be obeyed are on lines 5 and 1∅ and simply set the memory elements called I and S to zero. The table appears like:

| Line No. | S | C | N | I | Z | Branch |
|---|---|---|---|---|---|---|
| 5 | | | | ∅ | | |
| 1∅ | ∅ | | | | | |

After line 2∅ has been obeyed we have:



| Line No. | S | C | N | I | Z | Branch |
|---|---|---|---|---|---|---|
| 5 | | | | ∅ | | |
| 1∅ | ∅ | | | | | |
| 2∅ | | ∅ | | | | |

Line 3Ø picks up the first value from the data set and puts it in N, so:

| Line No. | S | C | N | I | Z | Branch |
|---|---|---|---|---|---|---|
| 5 | | | | Ø | | |
| 1Ø | Ø | | | | | |
| 2Ø | | Ø | | | | |
| 3Ø | | | 2 | | | |

Line 4Ø is an "If" statement, and so merely performs a test to see if N is negative. It isn't (it's currently 2) so the test is false, which we'll indicate by an "x" in the "branch" column and the branch to 1ØØ does not take place. When a test is true, and the branch does occur we will show this with a "√" in the "branch" column. Now we have:

| Line No. | S | C | N | I | Z | Branch |
|---|---|---|---|---|---|---|
| 5 | | | | Ø | | |
| 1Ø | Ø | | | | | |
| 2Ø | | Ø | | | | |
| 3Ø | | | 2 | | | |
| 4Ø | | | | | | x |

Line 5Ø asks the machine to take the contents of I, add the contents of C and put the result back in C. This should make us a bit suspicious because we know that I was not set up originally. So maybe adding line 5 wasn't such a good idea. Anyway, let's carry on with our simulated program run.

| Line No. | S | C | N | I | Z | Branch |
|---|---|---|---|---|---|---|
| 5 | | | | Ø | | |
| 1Ø | Ø | | | | | |
| 2Ø | | Ø | | | | |
| 3Ø | | | 2 | | | |
| 4Ø | | | | | | x |
| 5Ø | | Ø | | | | |

Of course, adding zero to zero has had no useful effect, and that should make us even more suspicious, so remembering that we are looking for typographical errors, we might suspect that I shouldn't be I at all, but 1, a pretty common slip, after all.

Now we start all over again with a new table, working on the new assumption that line 5 is unnecessary and line 5Ø reads

```
5Ø   LET C = C + 1
```

When the program reaches line 1∅∅ it will print the message "AVERAGE IS" followed by the value of S/C, which is zero!

So the program still doesn't work, but what is interesting is that now there is no error report from the 1000; we have introduced a new kind of error—a logical error. The 1000 can perform the operations we've asked for all right; it's just that having done so, it gets the wrong answer.

| Line No. | S | C | N | Z | Branch |
|---|---|---|---|---|---|
| 1∅ | ∅ | | | | |
| 2∅ | | ∅ | | | |
| 3∅ | | | 2 | | |
| 4∅ | | | | | x |
| 5∅ | | 1 | | | |
| 6∅ | | | | 2 | |
| 7∅ | | | | | √ |
| 3∅ | | | 1 | | |
| 4∅ | | | | | x |
| 5∅ | | 2 | | | |
| 6∅ | | | | 1 | |
| 7∅ | | | | | √ |
| 3∅ | | | 4 | | |
| 4∅ | | | | | x |
| 5∅ | | 3 | | | |
| 6∅ | | | | 4 | |
| 7∅ | | | | | √ |
| 3∅ | | | 6 | | |
| 4∅ | | | | | x |
| 5∅ | | 4 | | | |
| 6∅ | | | | 6 | |
| 7∅ | | | | | √ |
| 3∅ | | | −1 | | |
| 4∅ | | | | | √ |
| 1∅∅ | | | | | |

Let's have a look at the table we have generated. It is now fairly clear what the function of C is. Every time a new value is entered in N, the value in C is increased by one, so that when the branch to line 1∅∅ occurs, C contains the number of values entered altogether, in this case 4. But nothing at all has happened to S after it has been set to zero, and Z only contains the same values as N, but slight later. Perhaps S and Z should really be the same place, and since S is mentioned at line 1∅ first, let us assume that Z is a misprint for S. That means line 6∅ reads:

```
6∅   LET S = S + N
```

and the table becomes:

| Line No. | S | C | N | Branch |
|---|---|---|---|---|
| 1∅ | ∅ | | | |
| 2∅ | | ∅ | | |
| 3∅ | | | 2 | |
| 4∅ | | | | x |
| 5∅ | | 1 | | |
| 6∅ | 2 | | | |
| 7∅ | | | | √ |
| 3∅ | | | 1 | |
| 4∅ | | | | x |
| 5∅ | | 2 | | |
| 6∅ | 3 | | | |
| 7∅ | | | | √ |
| 3∅ | | | 4 | |
| 4∅ | | | | x |
| 5∅ | | 3 | | |
| 6∅ | 7 | | | |
| 7∅ | | | | √ |
| 3∅ | | | 6 | |
| 4∅ | | | | x |
| 5∅ | | 4 | | |
| 6∅ | 13 | | | |
| 7∅ | | | | √ |
| 3∅ | | | −1 | |
| 4∅ | | | | √ |
| 1∅∅ | | | | |

We now get printed:

```
AVERAGE IS 3.25
```

which is correct!

The process I have been describing is called "dry running" the program, and it is a common way of searching for errors. Of course, it isn't always necessary to include all the details I have shown in a dry run program table (for example, the line numbers have not been very useful to us in this case) and it often isn't necessary to complete a table before the light dawns, but I think you can see that it is a nice way of forcing you to think in the strait-jacketed way the machine does, and at the same time giving a clear view of the way the program runs.

Now you may say "all this is very well, but who is going to make typographical errors of this type keying in programs?"

The answer is that it happens all the time, for a number of reasons. First, if you copy a program from a magazine, there is the possibility that the error is present on the printed page. Second, you may easily make the odd keying error in a long program—I for 1, letter O for zero, 2 for Z and so on. Third, even when you are writing a program yourself you can make an error which is equivalent to a typographical error.

For example, suppose you call a variable B3 at the beginning of a program. You write the program over several days, tinkering a bit here, modifying a line there. At the end of this time you need to write a few more lines using this variable, which you remember quite well was called B2, so you don't bother to check.

You don't think it can happen? Wait till you've been programming for a few months.

The 1000 can draw things. Once it knows what to draw, it can move it around. Once it can move it around, the operator can control the movement through the keyboard. Particularly if you want to write computer game programs, you'll need to know something about

# GRAPHICS

An extremely attractive feature of computers is that they can draw pictures—with enough hardware, beautiful and intricate multicolored pictures. And while the 1000 is rather more limited, it has enough capabilities to provide a stimulating introduction to computer graphics.

The section of this book on *plotting* describes one way of using the computer to draw; but there we were thinking of rather academic things like rectangles. By using the PRINT facility, it is possible to draw objects with more visual appeal.

## THE "PRINT" INSTRUCTION

The fundamental instruction here is PRINT X$ where X$ is a character or a string of characters. It's almost self-explanatory. If you experiment with PRINTing, however, you will soon find that this instruction alone gives you little control over *where* a given character is printed: the machine starts every such instruction at the left of screen on the next available line, which isn't always what you want.

PRINT AT X,Y takes care of this. Much as for PLOT, the screen should be thought of as divided into squares, labelled with two coordinates X and Y. But there are several differences. First, the squares are twice as large. This means there are half as many each way; a quarter of the total altogether. Next, the coordinate numbering system is quite different—and more straightforward. The first number, X, is a *line* number on the screen; it runs from Ø at the top to 21 at the bottom of the area available for PRINTing. The second, Y, is a *column number* giving the dis-

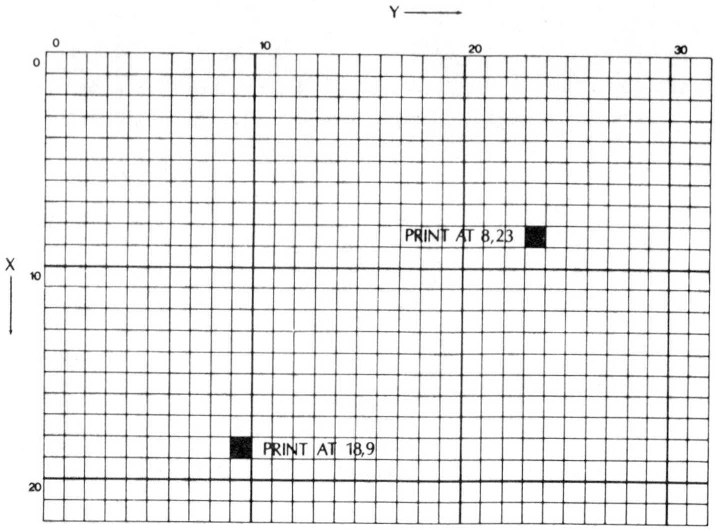


Figure 11

tance along a line (that is, horizontally), and running from ∅ to 31. Figure 11 shows this system in more detail.

Suppose you want to print the graphics character ▒ in the middle of the screen. The exact middle can't be achieved; but the square in line 11 and column 15 is pretty close. So you would write

```
1∅   PRINT AT 11,15;"▒" .
```

Note the semicolon (;) which is needed to tell the computer to run what it thinks of as *two* instructions together: move to 11,15; PRINT something.

By fitting several graphics characters together you can achieve more interesting effects. The most direct way to do this, by using large numbers of PRINT ATs, uses up precious memory the way a Cadillac uses petrol; but for the moment let's not worry about efficiency: only the principle is important. Try this program:

```
1∅   PRINT AT 1∅, 1∅; " ███▀▀▀▀ "
2∅   PRINT AT 11,8; " ▒█▒█▒█▒ "
3∅   PRINT AT 12,8; " ▐OOOCO▌ "
```

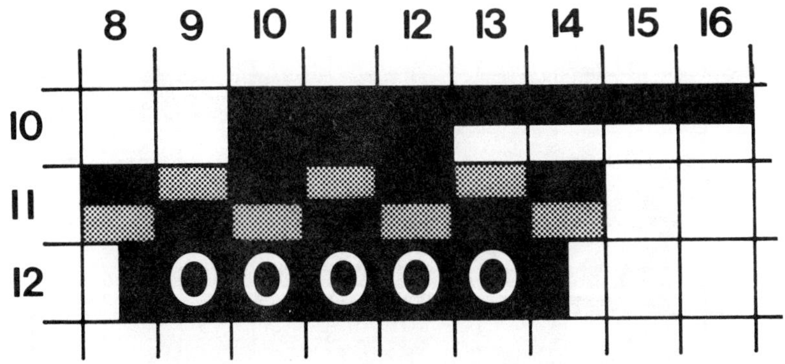


Figure 12

It should remind you of something of a military nature. (If not, blame my poor design.)

When printing graphic designs like this, a useful approach is to draw the design on squared paper, and number the lines and columns; this makes it easier to read off the required instructions. The above program is obtained by this process from Figure 12.

The 1000 has 21 special graphics characters (numbers 1-1∅ and 128–138; (22 if you count the blank space, character number ∅) in the character set (see *Manual,* page 63). But you can make good use of other characters too (as in the above example). Inverse video (white on black) characters are especially useful in this connection.

## CHANGING POSITION

Having worked out how to PRINT in a chosen position on the screen, it's not hard to modify the program so that you can PRINT the same graphics at any position you choose. The tank (yes, that's what it was supposed to be) above sits on line 12 with its left-hand edge in column 8. If we want to draw it sitting on line A with its left-hand edge in column B, we just renumber the lines and columns in the picture to achieve this effect (see Figure 13).

From this we can read off the new program:

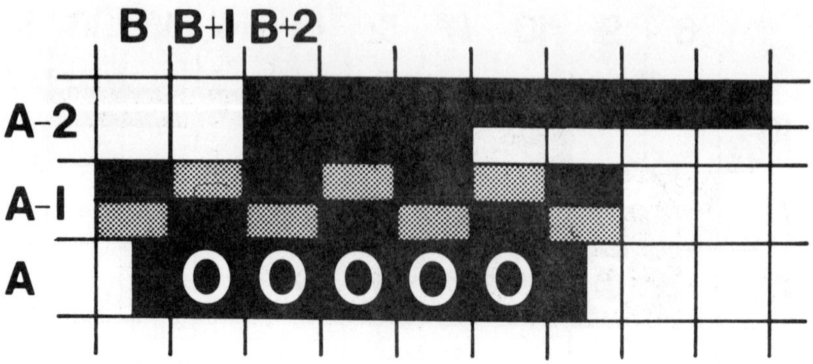


Figure 13

```
1Ø   PRINT AT A − 2,B + 2; "███▀▀▀▀"
2Ø   PRINT AT A − 1,B; "▒▒▒▒▒▒▒"
3Ø   PRINT AT A,B; "▐00000▌"
```

Of course this won't run unless you tell it the value of A and B in a previous piece of program. It also won't run if it encounters values of A and B that make the picture run off the edge of the screen. Looking at the left edge, that means B must be Ø or more; at the right, we need B + 9 to be 31 or less, that is, B = 22 or less. Similarly A must be 2 or more, and 21 or less.

The great advantage of thinking generally, like this, is that we can draw our tanks all over the place on the screen, just by specifying A and B. Here are some samples: tack them on to the lines 1Ø–3Ø above (the line numbers will automatically be ordered by the 1000) and run them, to see what you get.

```
(a)  1    LET B = 7
     2    FOR A = 2 TO 21
     4Ø   NEXT A
(b)  1    LET A = 15
     2    FOR B = Ø TO 22
     4Ø   NEXT B
(c)  1    LET A = 2 + 15*RND
     2    LET B = 2Ø*RND
     4Ø   GOTO 1
```



(BREAK this to put it out of its misery!)

Once you've learned about subroutines you'll be able to find all sorts of uses for this ability to draw a given shape in an arbitrary position. The next section describes one common circumstance in which this might be used.

## MOVING GRAPHICS

Suppose you want the tank to move across the screen from left to right. Program (b) above almost does this, except that it leaves a trail of rear ends of tanks behind it as it goes. You *can* get rid of these by overprinting blank spaces; but the nicest way is to use an "invisible border" which does this automatically. Change lines 1∅–3∅ like this:

```
1    LET A = 15
2    FOR B = ∅ TO 21
1∅   PRINT AT A - 2,B + 2; "□███▀▀▀▀"
2∅   PRINT AT A - 1,B; "□▀▄▀▄▀▄▀"
3∅   PRINT AT A,B; "□▐█OOOOO▌"
4∅   NEXT B
```

Note the blank spaces added at the front of each graphic line. (To avoid running over the edge, we make B run only up to 21 in line 2.)

The border of blanks is not visible on the screen; but the way the computer prints out characters means that these blanks are printed on top of that awkward "trail", blotting it out. (An old saying has it that foxes erase their tracks with their tail: so does our tank, but its tail is invisible.)

If we want to be able to reverse the position of the tank, then we need an invisible border at the right end too. To move it upwards, we need a border below it; to move downwards, a border above. To move in all directions (by varying A and B accordingly) we put the border all the way round the edge of the tank, which means two more lines of blanks in rows A − 3 and A + 1.

### PROJECT



Write a program to make the tank move round and round the edge of a square, size 1∅ by 1∅, on the screen. Put invisible borders all round; work out how A and B have to vary; program that.

## KEYBOARD CONTROL OF MOVEMENT

Now we can draw things that move around as we wish, it's possible to use the keyboard to direct the movements from outside the program.

The clumsy way to do this is to write the program as a loop, and to input something from the keyboard. This holds everything up, moving display and all, until the keys are pressed.

Better is the INKEY$ instruction. A program line like

```
1∅   LET C$ = INKEY$
```

tells the machine to see which key is being pressed, and assign to the string variable C$ the corresponding character. By playing tricks with that character, you can do all kinds of things.

For example, let's direct that tank either to left or right, using keys 5 for left and 8 for right. (This is useful for reminding *you*, because of the arrows on those keys; but it's *not* necessary to press SHIFT and actually input the arrows.) What do we do? We tell the machine to read the INKEY$; and adjust the print position according as this is 5 or 8. Like this:

```
1    LET B = 15
2    LET A = 12
3    LET C$ = INKEY$
6    IF C$ = "5" THEN LET B = B - 1
7    IF C$ = "8" THEN LET B = B + 1
1∅   PRINT AT A - 2,B + 2; "□■■■▀▀▀▀□"
2∅   PRINT AT A - 1,B; "□▒▒▒▒▒▒▒□"
3∅   PRINT AT A,B; "□▐◙◙◙◙◙▌□"
4∅   GOTO 3
```

Note the invisible border at both edges. The trouble with this is that if you press the keys for too long, you can run off the edge of the screen. See if you can modify the program to prevent this, by adding lines something like IF A < ∅ THEN . . . something or other.

If you keep a key pressed, this program keeps responding, and the tank keeps moving. Sometimes this is a terrible nuisance; often what you really want is for the program to respond only to *changes* in the INKEY$, or at least to renewed pressings of it.

In such cases, modify line 3 to the following:

```
3     IF INKEY$ <> "" THEN GOTO 3
4     IF INKEY$ = "" THEN GOTO 4
5     LET C$ = INKEY$
. . . .
```

This has the effect of holding everything at line 3 if you're still pressing down the old key. When you let go, it moves to 4 and holds there. When you press a new key or repress the old one—away she goes!

WARNING: do be careful what you tell the machine to do with that INKEY$. You may only *want* to press keys giving numbers, and then to work out VAL INKEY$ which converts that number from a character to something you can actually use for arithmetical calculations. But to start the program you have to press ENTER—and sometimes the 1000 reads *this* as the INKEY$, tries to turn it into a number—and the program crashes. Or worse, if no keys are pressed, it does VAL (the empty string). This can be a trifle puzzling until you've realized. (You can protect against it by using suitable IF . . . THEN instructions; but this can use a lot of memory and isn't always feasible, at least not without the 16K RAM pack.)

## PRINT AND PLOT IN COMBINATION

In some programs you may need to use both PRINT and PLOT together for graphic displays. It is important to remember that PRINT AT X,Y and PLOT X,Y produce quite different results, because the X,Y refer to two very different coordinate systems on the screen. The Timex *Manual* has a diagram on page 67 showing both, and page 64 gives a mathematical formula for changing from one system to the other. But usually the easiest way to make the two kinds of command fit together properly is to make a rough sketch, on squared paper, of the region you want to draw graphics in; mark in both coordinate systems; and refer to this sketch while writing your program. It is often worth spending some time thinking about the structure of the program *before* sitting yourself at the keyboard. (Equally, if your first attempt goes wrong, it is often easier to debug by experimenting on the machine, instead of bashing your brains out. The knack is to allocate your time and effort to best effect.)

## PAUSE

The 1000 has a PAUSE command, which makes it wait for a specified period of time. This looks as if it would be very useful for moving graphics; say, to slow down something which would otherwise move too fast.

In fact, it's hopeless for this job, because *the screen flickers when PAUSE is used,* and it looks horrible. Try out the "clock" program on page 76 of the *Manual.* You'll never be tempted to use PAUSE again.

Instead of PAUSE, you can use a loop that does absolutely nothing except use up time:

```
300  FOR J = 1 TO 25
310  NEXT J
```

and adjust the 25 to give longer or shorter loops.

Sometimes what you want the computer to do depends on what's happened so far. In this case you use a technique known as

# BRANCHING

This section is about logic, and *conditional* statements, where what the computer has to do depends on various other things. For example, when going to the pictures, IF you are under 16 THEN you will not be let into an X-rated film. You can put similar conditions on what the computer does.

The instruction you use to do it is IF . . . THEN . . .—but what goes into the dotdotdots is important.

Let's write a program to tell whether a given number is odd or even. (''Big deal!'' I hear you cry, and fair enough; but as elsewhere in this it is the principles that count, not the actual result.)

Here goes.

```
1Ø   INPUT N
2Ø   IF N = 2*INT(N/2) THEN PRINT "EVEN"
3Ø   IF N <> 2*INT(N/2) THEN PRINT "ODD"
```

How does this work? Even numbers are those exactly divisible by 2. So N is even exactly when N/2 is an integer. That means taking INT leaves it the same, so N/2 = INT(N/2). And *that* is the same as N = 2*INT(N/2). So line 2Ø is a fancy way of saying

```
2Ø   IF N is even THEN PRINT "EVEN"
```

which makes reasonable sense to *us*—but not to poor old 1000, who has no idea what ''is even'' means until we tell him in the language he understands.

Just to drive this point home, we'll work out a few cases.

| N | 22 | 23 | 24 | 25 | 26 |
|---|---|---|---|---|---|
| N/2 | 11 | 11.5 | 12 | 12.5 | 13 |
| INT(N/2) | 11 | 11 | 12 | 12 | 13 |
| 2*INT(N/2) | 22 | 22 | 24 | 24 | 26 |

That should be enough to convince even the direst skeptic.

(In the same way, K divides N exactly—for whole numbers K,N—if and only if N = K*INT(N/K). This is a very useful thing to know.)

Perhaps the one other thing to point out is that in line 3∅ the symbol <> means "is not equal to". A lot of mathematicians would use ≠ but the 1000 prefers <>. Don't ask me why..

In general you do the same kind of thing. The crucial instruction takes the form

```
1∅   IF this THEN that
```

where "this" and "that" are statements. (In the line 2∅ above, "this" is "N = 2*INT(N/2)" and "that" is "PRINT "EVEN"".)

The "this" statement has to be something that the computer can recognize as either true or false. (IF STOP THEN . . . isn't terribly informative, but IF N = 1981 THEN . . . is.) If "this" is true the computer then goes on to do "that"; if "this" is false it *goes on to the next program line without doing "that"*.

Two particularly common types of conditional command follow.

## CONDITIONAL JUMPS

These take the form

```
1∅   IF this THEN GOTO n
```

where n is a line number. Instructions like this can be used to change horses in midstream—that is, alter the whole course of the calculation by moving away to another part of the program.

For instance, when calculating the square root of a number it's important to remember that negative numbers don't have any. So you avoid error messages by doing something like this:

```
10   INPUT N
20   IF N < Ø THEN GOTO 5Ø
30   PRINT N,SQR N
40   STOP
50   PRINT "SQUARE ROOT NOT DEFINED"
```

Note the STOP in line 4Ø. Why? Chop it out and see what happens!

In the same way, when using PRINT AT A,B, you can protect against A and B in unPRINTable ranges by using:

```
1ØØ   IF A < Ø THEN GOTO 1ØØØ
 11Ø   IF A > 21 THEN GOTO 1ØØØ
 12Ø   IF B < Ø THEN GOTO 1ØØØ
 13Ø   IF B > 31 THEN GOTO 1ØØØ
 15Ø   PRINT AT A,B;"*"
 16Ø   STOP
1ØØØ   whatever you think is a useful response . . .
etc.
```

We assume here that A,B are assigned in a previous bit of program.

Tack on the front

```
1Ø   INPUT A
2Ø   INPUT B
```

and then ask the machine to PRINT AT 999, −37 by setting A = 999, B = −37.

Make line 1ØØØread

```
1ØØØ   PRINT "IM NOT SO STUPID ANY MORE"
```

Is it?

If you think lines 1ØØ–13Ø look clumsy . . . they are. See the section below on LOGIC.

## CONDITIONAL ASSIGNMENTS

These take the form IF this THEN LET something. For instance, an alternative to the first program above is

```
1∅  INPUT N
2∅  LET A$ = "ODD"
3∅  IF N = 2*INT(N/2) THEN LET A$ = "EVEN"
4∅  PRINT A$
```

Here A$ has a dollar sign because it's not a number, but a *string* of characters (see STRINGS, page 97).

What is this program?

```
1∅  LET S = INT(2*RND)
2∅  IF S = ∅ THEN LET A$ = "HEADS"
3∅  IF S = 1 THEN LET A$ = "TAILS"
4∅  PRINT A$
```

Whenever you are writing a program, and what you want to do depends on certain things happening or not happening, start thinking about IF . . . THEN . . .

## LOGIC

A big subject, examined endlessly in learned treatises . . . but we don't need to know most of that. The 1000 can do logic—probably better than you or I can. Specifically, it can combine statements occurring in the "this" position of an IF this THEN that, by using AND, OR, and NOT.

Basic rules: p AND q is true only when p is true and q is true.
p OR q is true when p is true, or q is true, or *both*.
NOT p is true only when p is false.

The 1000 works out NOTs before ANDs and ANDs before ORs. It works out almost everything else you can think of before it does any of these. As a result, you don't often need brackets to make the order clear.



For instance, we can improve lines 1∅∅–13∅ above by

changing them to the single line

```
1∅∅  IF A < ∅ OR A > 21 OR B < ∅ OR B >
31 THEN GOTO 1∅∅∅
```

There are all sorts of marvellous ways to use 1000 logic, but they're complicated to explain and I haven't much space, so I'll reluctantly stop here. Chapter 7 of the Timex *Manual* will get you started, but it's by no means the whole story.

. . . but why not use the 1000 to debug itself?

# DEBUGGING III

In the last example we looked at, the debugging process was achieved by a considerable amount of hard graft on our part. It would be nice to get the machine, whose sole function so far has been to sit there smugly telling us the wrong answer, to do some of the work for us.

So the question is: what kind of things could the machine usefully tell us about the way it is executing a program? There are three main areas to consider:

(1) What values does the program get for its variables at various stages in its execution?
(2) Where does the program go? (i.e. what lines get executed and in which order?)
(3) How often does it go there? (i.e. how many times do particular lines or groups of lines get executed?)

Some machines provide automatic features for printing out at least some of this kind of information, but you can't have everything for $99 (yet!) so we have to build some extra statements into our programs to provide some of these details. Let's look at the headings above in turn.

## PRINTING VALUES OF VARIABLES


It's very easy to print out values of variables anywhere we want. All we have to do is to insert a PRINT statement at an appropriate place in the program. For example, in our averaging program we might insert a line 55:

```
55   PRINT C
```

which would allow us to trace the changes in the value of C as the program executes. (In fact it wouldn't be difficult to get the machine to provide a copy of the dry run table which we produced by hand—you might like to try it.)

The real problem here is to choose where to output intermediate values sparingly and sensibly, otherwise you just get reams of numbers which take as long to analyse as a hand-generated dry run.

In the case of the second run of the averaging program, you will recall that an error report was generated at line 1ØØ so we didn't get any values printed out. A sensible first step would be to include a line 95:

```
95   PRINT S,C
```

Don't forget that line 4Ø will need modifying:

```
4Ø   IF N < Ø THEN GOTO 95
```

Otherwise the new statement will never get executed. That will have the effect of confirming our suspicion that C contains zero, but little more.

Now we could insert line 65

```
65   PRINT C; I; N; S; Z
```

so that we get a complete list of all the variables (in alphabetical order for convenience) at the end of every loop. This will create a simplified version of the dry run table which will still show up the salient points.

Incidentally, here's a neat trick: in the process of program testing you may want to remove one of the new lines temporarily to avoid having too many values printed at once. This means typing the whole line in again later, or worse, as in the case of our line 95, editing another line as well, since line 4Ø will have changed back to

```
4Ø   IF N < Ø THEN GOTO 1ØØ
```



if line 95 is removed. There is no need to do this. Simply edit in a

REM at the beginning of any line you want to disable. Line 95 becomes:

```
95  REM PRINT S,C
```

Since it is now a remark the machine will ignore it, but branching to line 95 is quite legal! When we want the statement back again, all we do is edit out the REM. Of course, if you have only 1K of memory, extra REMs may be a luxury you cannot afford. The moral to this story is: buy the extra 16K!

## TRACING THE ROUTE

The simplest way of tracing the route a program has taken is to follow every line with a PRINT statement which simply prints out the line number just executed. For example, the averaging program would become:

```
1Ø  LET S = Ø
11  PRINT "1Ø"
2Ø  LET C = Ø
21  PRINT "2Ø"
3Ø  INPUT N
31  PRINT "3Ø"
etc.
```

Again, we run the risk of generating too much information and not being able to see the wood for the trees, so let's be more selective about this "tracing" procedure. The kind of question which a trace will answer well is "does the program branch when it's expected to?". This being the case, it makes sense to restrict our trace to regions where there are branches.

For instance, suppose that a routine in a program is to input a day of a month. Such a value must be within the range 1–31 so it would be good programming practice to make sure that the user has entered such a value before continuing. We might write a piece of code like:



```
5Ø  INPUT D
6Ø  IF D > Ø OR D < 32 THEN GOTO 2ØØ
```

```
7Ø   REM HERE IF INVALID DAY
.
.
.
2ØØ  REM HERE FOR A VALID DAY
.
.
.
```

The program doesn't behave as it should, so we insert a trace statement after lines 5Ø, 7Ø and 2ØØ:

```
5Ø   INPUT D
51   PRINT "*5Ø"
6Ø   IF D > Ø OR D < 32 THEN GOTO 2ØØ
7Ø   REM HERE IF INVALID DAY
.
.
.
2ØØ  REM HERE FOR A VALID DAY
2Ø1  PRINT "*2ØØ*";
.
.
.
```

We find that whatever input value we try, the resulting trace is always:

```
*5Ø* *2ØØ*
```

(I'm using asterisks so that trace line numbers cannot be confused with numbers printed out by the program. Any special character that takes your fancy will do.)

So the program cannot be made to get to line 7Ø. There is only one sensible conclusion: the condition D > Ø AND D < 32 is always met. Logically this is so—any number is either greater than zero or less than 32. What we should have said was:

```
6Ø   IF D > Ø AND D < 32 THEN GOTO 2ØØ
```



Confusing AND with OR is a common error, because of the

rather sloppy way we use these words in ordinary speech. In this case both conditions must be met before we have a valid day so the AND connective is required.

## PROGRAM PROFILES

A program profile shows how many times each line of a program has been executed. As usual, this is overkill, and we should be selective about the parts of a program we want to profile. It's easy enough to do. Suppose that we want to find out how many times line 42∅ of a particular program is executed. We set up a count to zero at the beginning of the program and then increment it by 1 every time line 42∅ is passed through:

```
  5   PC = ∅
  .
  .
42∅   A = A*(P - 1)
421   PC = PC + 1
  .
  .
8∅9   PRINT PC
81∅   STOP
```

Let's look at a concrete example. The following program is intended to accept a maximum of 2∅ values, terminated by a zero, and sort them into ascending order. Thus if the input sequence is:

```
3
8
1
4
2
∅
```

the resulting output should be



```
1
2
```

```
3
4
8
```

The zero should not appear since it is only a delimiter.

```
 1Ø  DIM A(2Ø)
 2Ø  FOR P = 1 TO 2Ø
 3Ø  INPUT A(P)
 4Ø  IF A(P) = Ø THEN GOTO 6Ø
 5Ø  NEXT P
 6Ø  LET N = P
 65  LET F = Ø
 7Ø  FOR P = 1 TO N
 8Ø  IF A(P) < A(P + 1) THEN GOTO 13Ø
 9Ø  LET T = A(P)
1ØØ  LET A(P) = A(P + 1)
11Ø  LET A(P + 1) = T
12Ø  LET F = 1
13Ø  NEXT P
14Ø  IF F = 1 THEN GOTO 65
15Ø  FOR P = 1 TO N
16Ø  PRINT A(P)
17Ø  NEXT P
```

The program doesn't quite do the job. (Key it in and try it.) In fact it gets into an endless loop.

So where to start looking? The first loop (2Ø–5Ø) looks harmless enough, and the final one (15Ø–17Ø) is just printing out the contents of the array, A. It seems sensible then to concentrate on the loop from 7Ø to 13Ø. It is clear from line 8Ø that sometimes all the statements in the loop are executed, and sometimes those from 9Ø to 12Ø are ignored. So we'll have two profile counts, C1 and C2, which count the number of times the loop is entered and the number of times the last part of the loop is executed, respectively.

We can achieve this with:



```
67  LET C1 = Ø
68  LET C2 = Ø
75  LET C1 = C1 + 1
```

```
125   LET C2 = C2 + 1
132   PRINT C1,C2
```

While we are at it, we might as well print out the contents of the array at the end of each loop because it is obvious that numbers are being shovelled about inside it and that very few other variables are being used at all. So:

```
134   FOR Q = 1 TO N      (because 1 TO N seems to be the
                           relevant chunk of the array)
135   PRINT A(Q);
136   NEXT Q
137   PRINT
```

Let's try a few data sets and see what happens; if we enter

```
3
6
1
8
5
Ø
```

we get:

```
6  4
3165ØØ
6  4
13ØØ56
6  2
1ØØ356
6  2
ØØ1356
6  2
ØØ1356
6  1
ØØ1356
6  1
ØØ1356
```



and so on, until memory runs out.

Well, it seems to be getting values in order but we've lost the

"8" and where did the pair of zeros come from? Also, it goes round the main loop 6 times consistently but the number of times round the subloop decreases steadily until it reaches 1, where it stays.

One of the zeros is obviously the delimiter, and the other one is an element of the array which is not set during the run, but is initialized to zero by the system. In other words, the program is dealing with two values too many. So let's rewrite line 6∅:

```
6∅   LET N = P - 2
```

and try yet again. Hope beats eternal . . .

We get

```
4      2
3165
4      2
1356
4      ∅
1356
1
3
5
6
```

It's progress of a kind: we've got rid of those zeros. But we still haven't got our 8 back.

It's hard to see how it can have got lost. Perhaps it's still there, but not being printed out. Where do we PRINT it? Lines 15∅–17∅. The range 1 TO N must be too small. Let's increase it by 1:

```
15∅   FOR P = 1 TO N + 1
```

And, of course, while we're at it, the trace in line 134 is presumably having the same problems. So let's fix that up too:

```
134   FOR Q = 1 TO N + 1
```



Ho hum; once more unto the breach, dear friends, once more . . .

This time we get (for the same data):

```
4   2
31658
4   2
13568
4   Ø
13568
1
3
5
6
8
```

Great! we've cracked it. It's doing the job perfectly. Or is it? Let's try:

```
3
5
2
1
5
Ø
```

This time we get:

```
4   3
32155
4   3
21355
4   2
12355
4   1
12355
4   1
12355
4   1
12355
 .
 .
 .
etc.
```

It's getting the right answer, but it never comes out of the loop. We notice that C2 never gets down to zero in this case so it's a fair bet that this is what terminates the program.

What decides whether the program enters the subloop or not? Line 8∅:

```
8∅   IF A(P) < A(P + 1) THEN GOTO 13∅
```

The difference between the two data sets is that the second has two identical values in it. Since 5 is not less than 5 the subloop will be executed whenever the pair of 5's is encountered. That's why the program always goes round the subloop once. Perhaps the question should be:

```
8∅   IF A(P) < = A(P + 1) THEN GOTO 13∅
```

This time everything works.

```
4    2
32155
4    2
21355
4    1
12355
4    ∅
12355
1
2
3
5
5
```

Now it works like a charm and we can take out the test lines.

I hope I have illustrated a couple of important points here. Firstly, we haven't needed to know exactly how the procedure works. If you've worked through this carefully, it's probably fairly clear by now; and a few dry runs would probably convince you that you understand it. (Dry runs are a good way of understanding how computer procedures work. I've often done a dozen or so on some obscure piece of code—someone else's, of course—before being really clear in my mind about what's going on.) Secondly, there is always a temptation to believe that when a program runs successfully for the first time, the job is done and there's time for a quick burger at Hamburger Heaven. As we've seen, the job is *not* done, because there may be other sets of data for which the program fails; and anyway, Hamburger Heaven closed an hour and a half ago, if time goes as fast for you as it does for me when I'm writing code.

# T/S-WORD

**Across**

2. In this place, headgear lacks a head (2)
7. Fundamental Manx monster in a carriage found throughout this book (5,7)
12. Bend ear to make a speech (5)
13. A number may be located in tone-generators (3)
15. Lace-girt monitor becomes triangularly associated (15)
16. Disturbed new party with a high card up its sleeve spread out (6)
18. See 8 down
19. Half a dozen round the French flintstone (5)
20. Current clergy with fifty years to follow? Precisely! (10)
21. Give value as symbol (6)
23. Inputs guardsmen a second short (7)
24. Alternative Operational Research (2)
27. Original mate goes round the periphery (6)
29. Punishment ships? (6)
31. A Danish programming language developed in the USA (3)
33. Crated, upset, found (6)
34. Sin (11) gets printed neatly (4,5)
35. Depart, docked deity! (2)
39. Numerical input—500 at a gate (4,5)
40. Slim featherweight object (5)
41. The Post Office shelter is strong (6)
42. Winds reverse the winder (5)
43. Spin, gone, remakes beginnings of games! (8)
44. Singular information—an American lawyer's stomach (5)



**Down**

1. Communist intellectual with whom it forms an array (6)
3. Seafood sounds good on a piano (4)

4. To reckon delightful—about a disarrayed thatch of hair! (7)
5. Philosophical computer language tops a figure made from combinations (6,8)
6. You can only do it with a ROM (4)
7. A lot of loaves. . . . 100 in a tub (5)
8. 18ac. This way—remains true. The other way—remains immobile (5,5)
9. She coos weirdly and takes by preference (7)
10. Haley's functions? (5)
11. Airborne sprite causes faults in electronic equipment (7)
13. In this system a gross is a century! (5,9)
14. Every 1000 needs one cuter leg clip arrangement (8,4)
17. Correct logical value . . . 1 (4)
22. In sum, furthermore . . . (2,8)
30. . . . this function is an offence! (3)
32. Nicest digit, choicest part (4,3)
36. Strangely like 3, 5, and 9 lightyears (5)
37. Chunks of digits—do computers eat in this manner? (5)
38. The smallest home computer possible? (4)

---

*Solution on page 152*

If you can break a job down into a number of identifiable subtasks, then a powerful weapon in the programmer's armory becomes accessible:

# SUBROUTINES

There's a story about mathematicians that could equally well apply to computer programmers (yes, they *are* different animals!). About boiling a kettle. First the mathematician is asked to describe the stages to make a cup of tea, when the kettle is hanging on the hook in the kitchen; so he says something like "Take the kettle off the hook, fill it with water, put it on the stove, light a match . . ." and so forth. Then he is asked to describe the steps needed to make a cup of tea when the kettle is standing on the kitchen table—and he answers "Hang the kettle on the hook and proceed as before".

What he's doing is using the first sequence of operations as a *subroutine*. Second time, he modifies the existing situation to make the subroutine applicable, and then uses it as if it were a single indivisible operation.

In computer jargon, a subroutine is a chunk of program that can be written in its own right, and used repeatedly as part of some larger program. Subroutines are a very civilized way of writing programs because they usually make it easier to see what's going on. It is also easier to debug a program written with subroutines, because it is possible to debug each on its own, and then just to check they link together properly.

The relevant command is GOSUB. It's like GOTO but much more versatile. It typically occurs in this sort of way:

```
1ØØ  GOSUB 5ØØ
11Ø  various other junk
. . .
5ØØ  do something
. . .
57Ø  RETURN
```

where, as usual, the small letters denote other bits of program. What this does is:

(a) On hitting line 1ØØ the program jumps to 5ØØ, *remembering where it came from.*
(b) It then executes 5ØØ, and whatever follows it, until it hits line 57Ø and is told to RETURN.
(c) It then goes back to the original line (here 1ØØ), and carries on with the *next* instruction after that.

Essentially this is like GOTO, except that the return to the starting point is automatic. The important feature, though, is that you can enter the same subroutine from *different* lines in the same program, and the computer still keeps track of which it came in by, and RETURNs to that one.

As an example, I'll give a blow-by-blow account of the writing of a program which

(d) Uses keys 5, 6, 7, 8 to move around the screen a cursor [P].
(e) Prints in place of the cursor any character input from the keyboard.

For this character input we'll need to use INKEY$. We'll read the current key using this, and assign that to a string variable A$. We want the program to respond only to newly pressed keys, as described on page 66; so we need a chunk of program in the form

```
1ØØØ   IF INKEY$ <>"" THEN GOTO 1ØØØ
1Ø1Ø   IF INKEY$ ="" THEN GOTO 1Ø1Ø
1Ø2Ø   LET A$ = INKEY$
```

(will become the subroutine)

The 1ØØØ's are used because this will be a subroutine and we want to tuck it well out of the way (although actually you can often save a few program lines by putting all subroutines at the *front* end and starting the run using GOTO and not RUN—but that's a refinement not worth going into detail here). To come back out of it we'll need the extra line

```
1Ø3Ø   RETURN
```

Next, to move that [P] cursor around, we have to . . . what?

Well, we're certainly going to need to know *where* to print it; so we'll invent two variables, A and B, which give the values of the row and column on which to PRINT it. To stop the whole thing crashing before we get properly started we'll need to assign values to these. The middle of the screen is a good place to start:

```
1Ø   LET A = 1Ø
2Ø   LET B = 15
```

Now, we want to use keys 5, 6, 7, 8 to modify A and B, thus moving the cursor around. Good old Subroutine above will read the keyboard; so the obvious thing to do next is

```
3Ø   GOSUB 1ØØØ
```

Now A$ will tell us which of 5, 6, 7, 8 has been pressed. We want to move the [P] around in the direction of the four arrows on these keys. (That's why we use them: the arrows are good mnemonics!)

Take a look at Figure 14, which shows position A,B and the four neighbours. Using the clues in the picture, we see that we want:

key 5 to change B to B − 1 and leave A alone,
key 6 to change A to A + 1 and leave B alone,
key 7 to change A to A − 1 and leave B alone,
key 8 to change B to B + 1 and leave A alone.

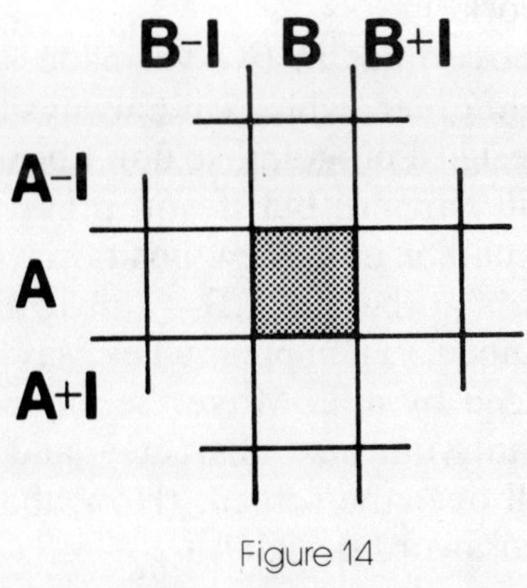


Figure 14

Here's one way:

```
4Ø  IF A$ = "5" THEN LET B = B − 1
5Ø  IF A$ = "6" THEN LET A = A + 1
6Ø  IF A$ = "7" THEN LET A = A − 1
7Ø  IF A$ = "8" THEN LET B = B + 1
```

Having moved the cursor, we'd like to see where it's gone:

```
8Ø  PRINT AT A,B; "[P]"
```

Now what? We want to input a character to print in place of this [P]. Subroutine again!

```
9Ø  GOSUB 1ØØØ
```

This time the machine reads the keyboard, assigns A$ the value it finds there (which is whatever we press, A, B, C, D, . . . , 7, 3, >, . . . ), and returns to *the next line after line* 9Ø. And we want this to tell it to print the character it's found:

```
1ØØ  PRINT AT A,B; A$
```

Nearly done now. So far this all works only once. We want to go back to the front and start again—but keeping the new A,B, *not* resetting to 1Ø and 15. That's easy:

```
11Ø  GOTO 3Ø
```

(3Ø then immediately sends it to 1ØØØ again. Why won't 11Ø GOSUB 1ØØØ work?)

Write all the above lines in (we've made sure the numbers work out in the right order, which isn't always the case first time round when you design a program, so don't be misled!) and press RUN. Nothing will happen; but if you press any of 5, 6, 7, 8 you'll see the [P] cursor in its new position. (If you press anything else, it appears at the old A,B—a programming bonus we hadn't actually planned.) Then press a key, say T. The [P] disappears, to be replaced by a T. Move the cursor (now invisible) using 5, 6, 7, 8; print your next character; and keep going. You can draw words all over the screen. (How about a program for computer-aided crossword design?)

To avoid crashing at the edges of the screen, a bit of user protection is a good idea:

```
75   IF A < Ø OR A > 21 OR B < Ø OR B > 31 THEN GOTO 3Ø
```

and no doubt you can think of refinements.

PROJECT

Instead of the INKEY$ subroutine, generate both 5, 6, 7, 8 inputs and the PRINTable characters at random; set the whole thing going and await developments. To print random characters use things like PRINT CHR$ INT(38 + 26*RND) which selects from the alphabet at random. (Why?)

Here's another example—an introduction to Computer Art. It draws random squares, black or shaded, until it runs out of memory or until you stop it with BREAK.

```
  1Ø   LET A = 1Ø*RND
  2Ø   LET B = 1Ø*RND
  3Ø   LET Q = 5*RND
  4Ø   LET R = 5*RND
  5Ø   LET K = INT(2*RND)
  6Ø   IF K = Ø THEN LET M$ = "■"
  7Ø   IF K = 1 THEN LET M$ = "▒"
  8Ø   GOSUB 1ØØØ
  9Ø   GOTO 1Ø
1ØØØ   FOR I = A TO A + Q
1Ø1Ø   FOR J = B TO B + R
1Ø2Ø   PRINT AT I,J;M$
1Ø3Ø   NEXT J
1Ø4Ø   NEXT I
1Ø5Ø   RETURN
```

PROJECT

Remember the program for PLOTting open or closed rectangles (page 43)? The program for closed rectangular blocks was much shorter than the one for open rectangles. Using subroutines you can shorten the program (at the expense of increased PLOTting time) as follows.

(1) Write a routine to PLOT or UNPLOT a rectangular block of specified size and position, according as a variable T is 1 or ∅.

(2) Use this as a subroutine in a program which PLOTs out a rectangular block of given size and position, and which then (if so instructed) uses the *same* subroutine to UNPLOT a smaller block inside, leaving just a hollow rectangle.

Somewhere in the middle you'll need lines like

```
27∅  IF T = 1 THEN PLOT X,Y
28∅  IF T = ∅ THEN UNPLOT X,Y
```

(In fact you can omit the characters "=1" and "=∅" here. Why?)

There is one quirk of this method. For just *one* rectangle PLOTted, it produces the same display as the original program would have done. Is this true if you use it repeatedly, without clearing the screen, to PLOT several rectangles?

## PROJECT: GRAPHIC DICE

Generate a random number between 1 and 6 using INT(1 + 6*RND). Depending on what this number, say N, is, print out N dots spaced on the screen just like they are on a die, near the centre of the screen. If ENTER is pushed, repeat this.

To do this, invent a subroutine for each of the six possibilities. If the subroutine for N is written starting at line (say) 5∅∅ + 1∅∅*N (that is at 6∅∅, 7∅∅, etc.) and ends well before the next one starts, you can cheat and use GOSUB 5∅∅ + 1∅∅*N to avoid complicated conditional jumps. But you do need six separate RETURN commands. . . .

For the ENTER repeat, use a line asking for an input character INPUT K$; follow it by a GOTO command sending everything back to the beginning. K$ isn't used for anything; but the machine waits for it, gets ENTER, and carries on to the GOTO. Get it?

# DEBUGGING IV

How do we prove conclusively that a program does precisely what it was written to do? I don't want to get involved in too complicated a philosophical discussion (because that's where we are headed) but, broadly, it's a bit like asking an astronomer whether the sun will rise tomorrow. If he is very pedantic he might answer that the earth has been going round the sun for a long time now and we have a body of physical laws which suggest that it will continue to do so in a regular way, and that the smart money would be on this continuing to be the case tomorrow; but he would add that he has no way of knowing whether our physical laws are right and that what we have observed for thousands of years might in fact be a manifestation of a much more complex law whose effect, tomorrow, might be to reverse the direction of the earth's rotation or to take it out of orbit completely.

By analogy, because a program behaves correctly for the first thousand sets of data input to it, there's no absolute guarantee that it will work for the thousand and first. In fact, bugs often don't become apparent until months or even years after a program has been apparently successfully completed and has been run without problems dozens or even hundreds of times. This isn't really surprising; after all, it's the conditions which occur least often that the programmer is most likely to overlook.

Here's an example:

We are writing a suite of programs for the Nether Hopping Electricity Board to handle their customer accounts. They explain to us that there are two rates, A and B. On the A rate the consumer pays a quarterly standing charge of $15 and then pays for units used at a rate of 4 cents per unit. On the B rate the consumer pays no standing charge and pays 7 cents per unit. So we write a piece of code like:

```
1ØØ   INPUT T$
1Ø5   INPUT UNITS
11Ø   IF T$ = "A" THEN GOTO 3ØØ
12Ø   IF T$ = "B" THEN GOTO 14Ø
13Ø   GOTO 5ØØØ
14Ø   LET BILL = 7*UNITS/1ØØ
15Ø   PRINT BILL
16Ø   GOTO 1ØØ
3ØØ   LET BILL = 15 + 4*UNITS/1ØØ
31Ø   PRINT BILL
32Ø   GOTO 1ØØ
. . .
5ØØØ  PRINT "INVALID RATE"
5Ø1Ø  STOP
```

OK. I know the code could be more efficient, and that we would actually need some more information like the consumer's name and account number, but you get the basic idea.

So we test this piece of code and it works fine and we go away muttering that it is a waste of our remarkable talents to be given Noddy programs like that to write.

And it does work fine; for years; and then one day it prints a bill for $0.00. Of course, nobody notices because it's one of thousands of bills and anyway it's probably enveloped automatically. The recipient is puzzled and probably amused by the bill because it shows how stupid computers are but there seems no point in taking any action so he throws the bill away. Unfortunately, we wrote another program in the same suite which stores the date that each bill was despatched, and if it does not receive confirmation that the bill has been paid within 28 days, it prints a final demand notice. This time the recipient is more irritated than amused but he just consigns it to the waste paper basket, as before. At this point things start to go visibly wrong. The routine which checks the delay between presentation of the account and payment issues an order to the maintenance department to cut off the consumer when he still hasn't paid after 6Ø days.



What's happened? Easy!! The consumer is an old-age pensioner who has taken advantage of one of the long winter break packages that the travel companies offer to senior citizens. He was out of the country for just over three months and used no electricity in a full account period. He is also an unusually frugal user of electricity so he's on rate B. That's why the system printed out a request for zero payment, and of course it won't happen very often because very few people will be away from home for that long, and rate B users are likely to be thin on the ground, too. For the problem to occur, the consumer has to fit both conditions.

Once seen, the bug is easily squashed:

```
145   IF BILL = ∅ THEN GOTO 1∅∅
```

so that the PRINT statement is avoided. This problem is supposed to have occurred in an early computer system, although whether it's a folk tale I wouldn't like to say. In any event, I think it illustrates neatly how a bug can lie dormant almost indefinitely.

The moral is: when you invent data to test a program, don't do so at random. Choose values at and close to branch values in the program. If a statement says:

```
3∅5   IF U < 3∅ THEN GOTO 5∅∅
```

then run a test with U at 29.999 and another at U = 3∅ and another at U = 3∅.∅∅∅1. You may have meant:

```
3∅5   IF U < = 3∅ THEN GOTO 4∅∅
```

If you only test at U = 15 and U = 16∅ you won't notice the error.

Make sure test data have been chosen so that every section of the program gets executed at some time. And of course, make sure you know exactly what the answer should be for each set of test data.

Computers aren't just number-crunchers. They can crunch characters too; that is, manipulate symbols.

# STRINGS

A *string* is a sequence of *characters*. The characters are listed on pages 137–143 of the *Manual*, and each has a CODE which we'll talk about in a moment.

Here's a string:

STRINGSTRINGSTRINGSTRINGSTRING.

Here's another one:

AB334*./>>>><<−B+++++QQJ.

(If you type the full stops, they're part of the string too!)

A string can be only one character long, such as <, or even *no* characters long!

To assign a string variable, you have to put inverted commas around the string:

```
1Ø   LET A$ = "STRINGSTRINGSTRINGSTRINGSTRING"
```

Every string variable must be a single letter followed by the $ sign. For a string no characters long, LET A$ = ".3" works.

Strings will sit up and beg if you know how to ask them to. Consider a single character string like

3

This can be thought of as:

(a) a number, 3
(b) a string, "3"

and you can switch from one to the other in various ways. Suppose we really do think of it as a string, and assign it:

```
1∅   LET A$ = "3"
```

Suppose you want to work out 3 + 5. It's no good asking the 1000 to do this:

```
2∅   LET B = A$ + 5
3∅   PRINT B
```

It won't work—try it if you don't believe me. Why not? The foolish beast has been told that 3 is to be considered a *string,* and it doesn't know it's a *number* too. But—ahah—we can *convert* it to a number using VAL. Try

```
2∅   LET B = VAL A$ + 5
3∅   PRINT B
```

In general, given a string which happens to be an arithmetical expression:

```
1∅   LET A$ = "2 + 2 + 5*3"
```

the machine does not know it can be worked out as a number; it just thinks of it as a sequence of *characters*

```
2 + 2 + 5*3
```

For instance, you can pick out the 6th character in it:

```
2∅   PRINT A$(6)
```

and get * as your answer. (This can be useful: as an arithmetical expression it equals 19 which doesn't *have* a sixth character.) But if you *want* to convert it to a number, then

```
2∅   PRINT VAL A$
```



will come up with 19 as your answer.

You can convert a number to a string in two ways. First, by putting inverted commas around it, "3336" or whatever. BUT if you're inside a program, and are working out A + B or whatever, which *is* 3336, it's no good writing "A + B" and hoping to get "3336" in there: what you get is the three-character string

A + B

which is rather different.

CHR$ converts a number between ∅ and 255 into a single character according to the list of codes in the *Manual* on pages 137–143. For instance, CHR$ 12 is the pound sign £. Some numbers aren't used.

CODE goes the other way: CODE "£" is 12. If you try CODE "£335/H" you still get 12: it only looks at the first character.

LEN tells you how long a string is.

By far the most interesting feature of strings is that you can chop bits out of them, called *substrings*. The instruction

```
A$ (3 to 7)
```

picks out the string consisting in turn of the 3rd, 4th, 5th, 6th, and 7th characters in A$. So if A$ = "STRINGSTRINGSTRINGSTRINGSTRING" then A$ (3 TO 7) = "RINGS". You can use any numbers in place of 3 and 7. And A$ (5) picks out just the 5th character—here "N".

For instance, suppose you want to input a number between 1 and 7 and say which day of the week that gives (taking 1 as Sunday, 2 as Monday, etc.) A clumsy way would be

```
1∅  INPUT N
2∅  IF N = "1" THEN PRINT "SUN"
3∅  IF N = "2" THEN PRINT "MON"
. . .
```

until all seven days are accounted for.

But, using substrings:

```
1∅  LET A$ = "SUNMONTUEWEDTHUFRISAT"
2∅  INPUT N
3∅  PRINT A$(3*N - 2 TO 3*N)
```

does the same job in 5 fewer lines; see DAYFINDER, page 142.

You can stick strings end to end using + to join them, like this:

"HOT" + "DOG" = "HOTDOG"

or order them "alphabetically" using <. Consult the *Manual,* and experiment. Careful use of strings can often save a lot of space.

PROJECT

Write a program to take a name and find its initials. That is, FREDERICK HIERONYMOUS BLOGGS should turn into FHB; or GINORMOUS ELECTRONIC CORPORATION into GEC.

Hint: INPUT it as a character string, spaces and all. Run along it looking for spaces; take the first letter and each letter that follows a space, add them all together, PRINT the result.

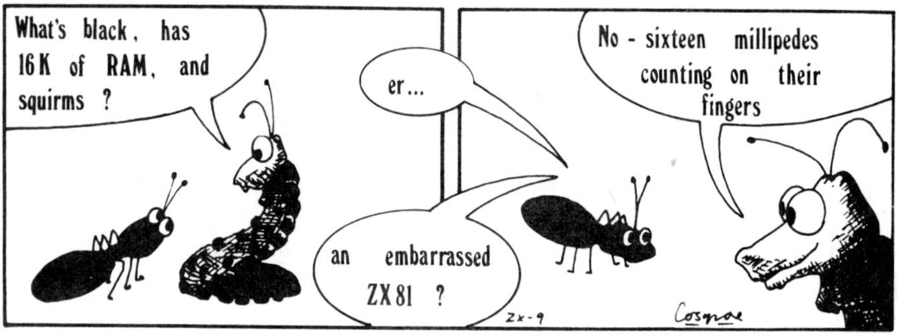

# GRAPH PLOTTING

You've probably met the idea of a *graph* specified by coordinates; but just in case, let's recap. Start with two lines, the x-axis and the y-axis, at right angles to each other. We can mark off distances x and y along these (marking negative numbers to the left on the x-axis and downwards on the y-axis) and use these two distances to specify a point with *coordinates* x and y. It's just like pixels (Figure 15).

If we now imagine x varying along the x-axis, and the value of y changing in some way that depends on x, then the point with coordinates (x,y) will move too; and it generally traces out a

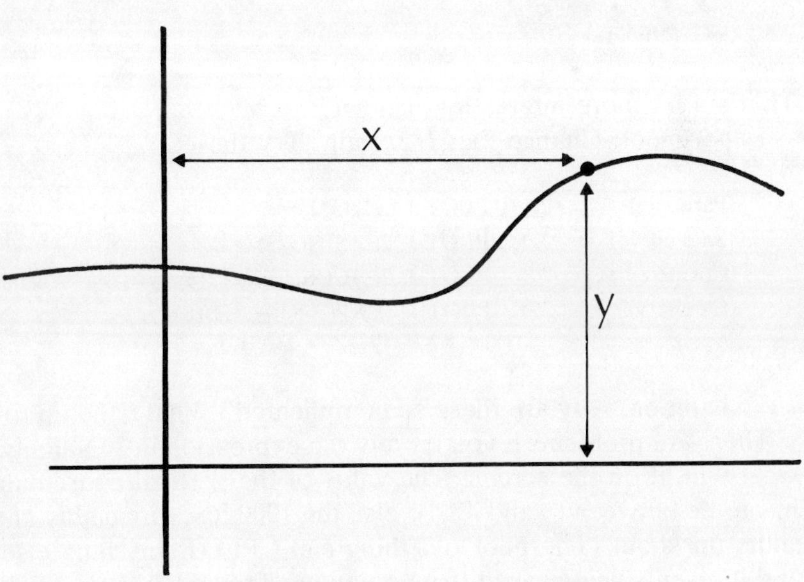


Figure 15 Coordinates for curve-plotting

*curve*. If you give a formula for how y depends on x, say $y = x^2 - 3$, then you give a formula for that curve. (This idea, due to Descartes in 1637, lets you use algebra to study geometric curves: it's the starting-point for calculus.)

Using PLOT instructions we can draw similar curves—but only coarsely, because we have only 64 values of x to play with.

Enough of this theory: let's try one.

```
1∅   FOR J = ∅ TO 63
2∅   PLOT J,J/2
3∅   NEXT J
```

You should get a sort of staircase of pixels climbing up the screen from lower left to top right. It's trying to draw a straight line, but this is the closest it can get, because of the coarseness of the vertical positions available. A mathematician would call this the graph of the function $y = x/2$.

You can modify this to give an endless variety of graphs, just by changing J/2 to some other expression involving J. For instance, to plot the square root of J as a function of J all you have to do is change the J/2 to SQR J, getting:

```
1∅   FOR J = ∅ TO 63
2∅   PLOT J, SQR J
3∅   NEXT J
```

That's a bit more interesting, isn't it?

Experiment. Change that J/2 again. Try these.

```
(Parabola)        2∅   PLOT J, .∅1*J*J
(Sine curve)      2∅   PLOT J, 2∅*SIN(J/3) + 2∅
(Cosine curve)    2∅   PLOT J, 2∅*COS(J/3) + 2∅
(Catenary)        2∅   PLOT J, (EXP(.1*(J – 3∅))
                        + EXP(.1*(3∅ – J)))*1.5
```

. . . hang on, why are these so complicated? What *is* he up to?

There are problems if you try any old expression in J. Namely, what will fit on the screen. The value of the vertical coordinate has to be between ∅ and 43, or else the 1000 loses its paddy and shuts up shop. (The poor old thing can't PLOT anything else, and it resents being asked to.) So you need to adjust the *scale* to make things fit. You'll soon see why if you try

```
2∅   PLOT J, J*J
2∅   PLOT J, SIN J
2∅   PLOT J, COS J
2∅   PLOT J, EXP(J) + EXP(-J)
```

There are ways round this problem, of course—see below, under SCALE. But before you do, here are some more interesting functions that *do* fit, because we've carefully chosen them to.

```
2∅   PLOT J, EXP(-J/2∅)*SIN(J/2)*2∅ + 2∅
2∅   PLOT J, 2∅ + 2∅*COS SQR (1∅*J)
2∅   PLOT J, ABS(J - 3∅)
2∅   PLOT J, 2∅ + 15*LN(1 + ABS SIN (J*.5))
2∅   PLOT J, 3*ABS(J - 3∅)**.666
2∅   PLOT J, 1∅*ABS(J - 3∅)**.25
2∅   PLOT J, 4∅*EXP(-.1*(J - 3∅)*(J - 3∅))
```

To avoid writing complicated expressions, you can build up the formula in stages, like this:

```
2∅   LET T = J/6
25   PLOT J, 3∅ + .∅25*T*(T - 2)*(T - 4)*(T - 6)*(T - 8)*(T - 1∅)
```

## SCALE

For the moment we'll work just with functions defined for *positive* numbers and taking *positive* values: a good one to use is SQR, the square root. Take the graph-plotting program above, and change line 2∅ to the following in turn:

```
(a)  2∅   PLOT J, .5*SQR J
(b)  2∅   PLOT J, SQR J
(c)  2∅   PLOT J, 1.5*SQR J
(d)  2∅   PLOT J, 2*SQR J
(e)  2∅   PLOT J, 3*SQR J
(f)  2∅   PLOT J, 4*SQR J
(g)  2∅   PLOT J, 5*SQR J
(h)  2∅   PLOT J, 6*SQR J
```



You'll notice pretty quickly that in successive graphs, everything goes higher up the screen—and in fact, in (g), the machine stops because graph points start to go off the screen altogether. The greater the "something" in (something)*SQR J, the more the graph is stretched in the vertical direction. This "something" is a *scale factor,* and by adjusting it you can make graphs fit the screen neatly.

If the scale factor is too small, you get graphs that are so squashed up you can't see anything. Try

```
2∅   PLOT J, .1*SQR J
```

If the function you're plotting grows too large, you can get it back on the screen by adjusting the scale factor. For example

```
2∅   PLOT, J*J
```

goes off the screen because 7*7 = 49, which is already too big. In fact the largest number you need to plot is 63*63 = 3969. If you divide this by 1∅∅ you get 39.69, which fits neatly into the 43 that is permissible. So you get a nice graph provided you use 1/1∅∅ as the scale factor:

```
2∅   PLOT J,.∅1*J*J
```

There is a fairly obvious general rule which makes sure the scale factor is chosen suitably. Suppose that the largest value the function takes as J runs from ∅ to 63 is M (for maximum). Then with scale factor S, everything is fine provided S*M is no larger than 43—and preferably close to it so that the graph isn't too squashed. In particular, you can make S*M = 43, by setting S = 43/M. (For round figures 4∅/M may be better; and you need a reasonable estimate for M rather than an exact number.)

In fact, you could write a program to work out M. Suppose we stick to the J*J function; then this will do the trick:

```
1∅   LET M = ∅
2∅   FOR J = ∅ TO 63
3∅   LET Q = J*J
4∅   IF Q > M THEN LET M = Q
5∅   NEXT J
```



As it stands this won't PLOT the graph, though; so now you add the plotting routine:

```
6∅   FOR J = ∅ TO 63
7∅   PLOT J, (43/M)*J*J
8∅   NEXT J
```

One defect: you have to do all the calculations *twice*. This is hard to avoid efficiently, unless you know *which* J gives the largest value for J*J. In this case J = 63 obviously does, but it's not always easy to see in advance. (You *can* dimension a vector V(I) of size 64, store the values of J*J as V(J + 1), and use these for the PLOT; but vectors and arrays take up a lot of memory! See the *Manual* for further information on vectors and arrays.)

As well as scaling the vertical axis, you can scale the horizontal axis. The function SQR J or J*J doesn't show this very vividly, so I'll use 2∅ + 2∅*SIN J, which does. Try the following:

```
2∅   PLOT J, 2∅ + 2∅*SIN(.∅5*J)
2∅   PLOT J, 2∅ + 2∅*SIN(.1*J)
2∅   PLOT J, 2∅ + 2∅*SIN(.15*J)
2∅   PLOT J, 2∅ + 2∅*SIN(.2*J)
2∅   PLOT J, 2∅ + 2∅*SIN(.25*J)
```

This time the *horizontal* scale changes—but the scale factor acts rather differently (did you notice?). The greater the scale factor, now, the more the graph is squashed up in the horizontal direction: you get more wiggles in the curve. Why?

When J ranges from ∅ to 63, the number .∅5*J ranges from .∅5*∅ to .∅5*63, that is, from ∅ to 3.15.

When J ranges from ∅ to 63, .1*J ranges from .1*∅ to .1*63, that is ∅ to 6.3.

So, in the second case, *twice* the range of values gets squashed into the same horizontal space.

In fact, with a scale factor S—that is, using

```
2∅   PLOT J, 2∅ + 2∅*SIN(S*J)
```

you plot the range from ∅ to S*63 in the width of the screen. The greater S is, the larger the range, so the more squashed it becomes.

So, if you want to plot over a chosen range, say 1∅∅∅, then you want S*63 = 1∅∅∅, that is, S = 1∅∅∅/63. In general, if you want the range ∅ to N, you'll need a scale factor N/63.

To sum up:

$$\text{best vertical scale factor} = \frac{43}{\text{largest value being plotted}}$$

$$\text{best horizontal scale factor} = \frac{\text{top of range of values of variable}}{63}$$

### PROJECT

If you don't know what's going to look best, you can write an "interactive" program which lets you choose the two scale factors (via INPUT) and then plot the graph; if you don't like the result you run it again and change the scale.

Write such a program for the function 2∅ + 2∅*SIN(J).

Hint: if H is the horizontal scale factor and V the vertical, the operative program line is

```
2∅   PLOT J, V*(2∅ + 2∅*SIN(H*J))
```

## SHIFTING AXES

You may be wondering: "why all those 2∅ + 2∅*SIN J's?" Or maybe, "That's all very well, but what if the numbers are negative?" The answer is the same to both. The way to deal with negative numbers is to shift your axes, as Eric the Viking once said.

Try this program.

```
1∅   INPUT S
2∅   FOR J = ∅ TO 63
3∅   PLOT J, S + SQR J
4∅   NEXT J
```

Try inputting S = ∅, 5, 1∅, 15, 2∅, etc.

What you'll see is the same graph, but moving higher up the screen according to the value of S. There are two ways to think of this.

One is that you're plotting different functions, like 5 + SQR J or 1∅ + SQR J.

The other is that you're always plotting SQR J, but that the position of the x-axis on the screen changes. See Figure 16, which is pretty much self-explanatory.

To get a clear sine curve, for instance, you need to replace the SQR J above by 2∅*SIN(.1*J); and pick S to get everything central on the screen. S = 2∅ works beautifully; hence all those 2∅ + 2∅*SINs.

That gets the x-axis moving. To get the y-axis moving, you can change the range of J, say from −3∅ to 33 instead of ∅ to 63.

You can combine these shifts with scalings in both directions; and you don't have to keep the axes central—it's up to you. I did in fact write out a detailed specification of how to do it to get the best possible display on the screen for a given curve over a given range; then I took one look at the mass of algebra that I'd written, and chucked the lot away again. There are times when mathematics hides the wood behind the trees, and this is one of them.

Instead, I suggest you experiment, using this program.

```
1∅   INPUT A
2∅   INPUT B
3∅   INPUT C
4∅   INPUT D
5∅   LET U = −B/(A*2)
6∅   LET V = 21 − D/2
```

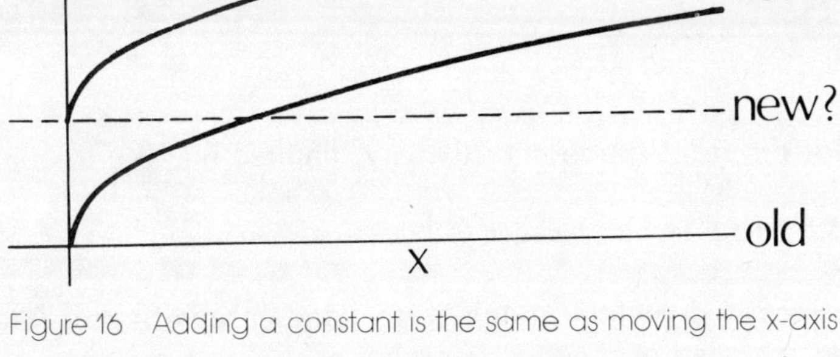


Figure 16  Adding a constant is the same as moving the x-axis

```
 7∅  PRINT AT V - 1,∅
 9∅  FOR J = ∅ TO 31
1∅∅  PRINT "-";
11∅  NEXT J
12∅  PRINT AT ∅,∅
13∅  FOR J = ∅ TO 2∅
14∅  PRINT TAB U - 1;"*"
15∅  NEXT J
16∅  FOR J = ∅ TO 63
17∅  PLOT J,C*SIN(A*J + B) + D
18∅  NEXT J
```

Here A, B, C, D shift axes and scale; while the x-axis is drawn as -------- and the y-axis as *********. I haven't protected against crashes if the function goes out of range—apart from laziness, this drives home the need to take care in choosing scale and position of axes.

(Try A = .2, B = −5, C = 1∅, D = 2∅. Negative B is generally necessary.)

## BAR CHARTS

For a display that is more attractive than a lot of square dots, you can draw vertical (or indeed horizontal, if you want) bars instead.

To do this, we change the program. Here's a typical case.

```
1∅  FOR J = ∅ TO 63
2∅  LET T = 2∅ + 2∅*SIN(.1*J)
3∅  FOR I = ∅ TO T
4∅  PLOT J,I
5∅  NEXT I
6∅  NEXT J
```

To plot different functions this way, change line 2∅ to

```
2∅  LET T = the function of J that you want.
```



This really does look much better; and care with presentation of data is a sign of a good programmer.

## PROJECTS

(1) Horizontal bars.
(2) Bars coming down from the top.
(3) Bars that start at the middle of the screen and go up or down according as the end is above or below the x-axis.

Sometimes numbers that look the same . . . aren't!

# DEBUGGING V

The kinds of bugs we've looked at so far have been of our own making, and have been reasonably easy to cure once we have seen them. There's another kind of bug which is caused by the design of the machine itself. It's not a design fault but a consequence of the way all computers are organized. It's to do with the precision with which computers store numbers. If we think about any common way of holding numbers it's obvious that there is a limit to the number of digits that can be held. A car mileage indicator, for example, can only hold 5 digits because it only has 5 "windows". It's just the same with a computer. Each number can occupy no more than a fixed number of "windows". However, each window does not represent a decimal digit. The internal machine code for numbers is quite different from the way we think about them, and I will not bore you with the gory details. The fact that there is inherent inaccuracy *and* a code conversion being employed means that the external representation of a number (as it is displayed on the screen) may not be quite the same thing as the internal representation. I'll give you an example of what I'm talking about from school logarithms. If you multiply 2 by 2 using logs you get:

| No. | Log. |
|---|---|
| 2 | Ø.3Ø1Ø |
| 2 | Ø.3Ø1Ø |
| 3.999 | Ø.6Ø2Ø + |

 i.e. $2 \times 2 = 3.999$!!

The combination of the fact that the logs are only accurate to 4 figures (i.e. they are only allowed to occupy 4 windows) and that a code conversion (number to logarithm, logarithm back to number) is taking place, creates the inaccuracy.

Here is a program which causes the same kind of problem:

```
1∅   FOR P = ∅ TO .3 STEP .∅1
2∅   LET Q = ATN(TAN(P))
3∅   IF P <> Q THEN PRINT P,Q
4∅   NEXT P
```

At line 1∅, we take the tangent of P and then immediately invert the process by taking the arctangent of the result. In other words, Q should contain the same value as P. So line 3∅ should never have the effect of printing P and Q because they are always equal. When the program is run we get the following output:

```
∅.∅2   ∅.∅2
∅.∅3   ∅.∅3
∅.∅4   ∅.∅4
∅.∅5   ∅.∅5
∅.∅7   ∅.∅7
∅.∅9   ∅.∅9
∅.11   ∅.11
∅.12   ∅.12
∅.13   ∅.13
∅.14   ∅.14
∅.16   ∅.16
∅.18   ∅.18
∅.2∅   ∅.2∅
∅.21   ∅.21
∅.22   ∅.22
∅.26   ∅.26
∅.28   ∅.28
```

This is a very strange result indeed, because the machine is not only printing out values, and so claiming they are different, but it is also printing them as if they were the same! What has happened is that the complex mathematical processes involved have led to slight inaccuracies in the internal representation of the numbers, which have accounted for the differences between P and Q. However, there are also inaccuracies involved in decoding the internal format back to the decimal numbers displayed on the screen so that they appear to be identical although the machine is adamant that they are not. Note that for some values the internal codes *are* identical: for ∅.∅6 and ∅.∅8, for example.

This kind of error can be extremely puzzling and sometimes the only way out of it is to allow a small error in the IF statement so that we have:

```
IF ABS(P − Q) <∅.∅∅∅∅∅1 THEN . . .
```

The ABS function is necessary because Q might be greater than P. For example, if P = 3.1 and Q = 3 then P − Q = −∅.1, which is less than ∅.∅∅∅∅∅1 so the condition would be met if the ABS function (which effectively chops off the minus sign) were not there. ABS(−∅.1) = ∅.1 which is greater than ∅.∅∅∅∅∅1 and so the condition is not met, which is what we wanted.

The internal organization of the 1000 is not something you usually need to worry about. But, if you want to, you can get the machine to tell you what it's doing — and you can change it to further your own ends.

# PEEK & POKE

I could probably write another book the size of this one on PEEK and POKE. And most of it would be far too technical to be useful. But it seems a shame to avoid these extremely important features altogether. By exploring PEEK and POKE you can really learn a great deal about the *way* computers operate. So, obviously, what you need is some idea of how to get started: how to talk the 1000 into giving away some of its innermost secrets.

On page 13 I mentioned that computers store information as sequences of Ø's and 1's. Each such Ø or 1 is called a *bit* (short for *b*inary dig*it*). You can think of a string of Ø's and 1's as a number in the *binary system,* which is just like the decimal system except that in place of units, tens, hundreds, thousands, etc. we use units, twos, fours, eights, and so on. In the Program Listings you'll find a program on binary/decimal conversion which explains this a little more.

We don't really need to know about binary; but we *do* need to recognize that computers work with *bits*. In fact, they generally carry their bits around in chunks, called *bytes*. One byte is a sequence of eight bits. So 1Ø11ØØØ1 and ØØ111Ø11 are typical bytes.

There are 256 possible different bytes; if you convert to decimal you get the numbers from Ø to 255. You may recognize these numbers: the CODEs of characters are numbers between Ø and 255. And indeed, each character is represented by exactly one byte.



A program (and some of the steps performed in carrying it out) is just a sequence of characters; so the machine can store it as a sequence of bytes. To make sure everything stays in the right order it gives each byte a reference number, called its *address*. So you should think of the program as living outside the machine in some form rather like

| Address | Byte |
|---|---|
| 1 | 11∅∅11∅∅ |
| 2 | ∅111∅∅∅∅ |
| 3 | ∅∅∅∅∅∅∅∅ |
| 4 | 111∅1111 |
| ..... | |

Unfortunately, the machine "architecture" makes a scheme like this a little too simple.

The 1000 consists of four microchips, known as the

ROM (Read Only Memory)
RAM (Random Access Memory)
CPU (Central Processing Unit)
SCL (Sinclair Logic Chip).

The ROM stores the BASIC interpreter; the RAM stores your program and anything that needs to be worked out while running it; the CPU does the arithmetic and the logic; and the SCL organizes how the others fit together.

We are not interested in the CPU or the SLC; but we *are* interested in the ROM and the RAM. And we can find out exactly which bytes are stored in which addresses in the ROM and RAM by using PEEK.

An instruction

```
PRINT PEEK 837
```

for example, will PRINT out the byte stored in address 837 (it's 2∅3, or 11∅∅1∅11 in binary). It prints out the corresponding decimal, in fact; so there's no harm in thinking of a byte as just a number between ∅ and 255.

For useful PEEKing, where should we look?

The ROM addresses run from ∅ to 8191. There are certainly some good reasons for PEEKing the ROM—you can find out how the 1000 tells the TV to PRINT a particular character, and play games (like printing it out four times the usual size) with this.

But more interesting are the RAM addresses. These start at 16384; and those up to 165Ø8 are set and used by the machine. Your program is placed in addresses 165Ø9 onwards. How far on depends on the length of the program, and whether you have the standard 2K RAM that comes built into the machine, or the extension 16K RAM.

To find out what's stored in the RAM, it's best to let the machine do the work. Here's a program that does this.

```
1ØØØ  LET Q = 165Ø8
1Ø1Ø  LET R = PEEK Q
1Ø2Ø  PRINT Q; "□□"; R; "□□"; CHR$ R
1Ø3Ø  LET Q = Q + 1
1Ø4Ø  GOTO 1Ø1Ø
```

I've used large line numbers because the idea is to put this after a program, and then to run it using

```
GOTO  1ØØØ
```

(*not* RUN, which will run the other program first!) to find out how that program is stored in the RAM.

Type this in; and also type in

```
1Ø  REM START
2Ø  PRINT AT Ø, 1Ø;"*"
```

Now hit GOTO 1ØØØ and watch. You'll get a print-out like this:

```
165Ø8    Ø
165Ø9    Ø
1651Ø   1Ø   ▒
16511    7   ▛
16512    Ø
16513  234   REM
16514   56   S
16515   57   T
16516   38   A
16517   55   R
16518   57   T
16519  118   ?
1652Ø    Ø
```

| 16521 | 2∅ | = |
|---|---|---|
| 16522 | 23 | * |
| 16523 | ∅ | |
| 16524 | 245 | PRINT |
| 16525 | 193 | AT |
| 16526 | 28 | ∅ |
| 16527 | 126 | ? |
| 16528 | | ∅ |
| 16529 | | ∅ |

What do we make of this?

Well, we can see our program—or most of it—building up in the third column. REM, S, T, A, R, T, . . . then PRINT,AT, . . . But there's some other junk too. The third column doesn't help us understand this; but the second does. For instance, in address 1651∅ we find 1∅ in the second column; in 16521 we find 2∅. These are obviously the *line numbers* from the program. They seem to have a ∅ in the previous address, and then possibly some more junk, and then another ∅. What about the ?'s? We can look them up in the *Manual,* Appendix. Address 16519 has the byte 118, which is ENTER. Address 16527 has 126, "number"—a cryptic statement, which no doubt refers to the way the 1000 stores its numbers internally.

So: we're going to have to puzzle out the numbers part more thoroughly; but we seem to be able to recognize where the program is. As a check, we can *carry on listing the contents of RAM* by pressing CONT and then ENTER. (This makes our little program in lines 1∅∅∅–1∅4∅ an absolute godsend.) We get another screenful of stuff:

| 1653∅ | ∅ | |
|---|---|---|
| 16531 | ∅ | |
| 16532 | ∅ | |
| 16533 | 26 | , |
| 16534 | 29 | 1 |
| 16535 | 28 | ∅ |
| 16536 | 126 | ? |
| 16537 | 132 | ▜ |
| 16538 | 32 | 4 |
| 16539 | ∅ | |
| 1654∅ | ∅ | |

```
16541      ∅
16542     25   ;
16543     11   ``
16544     23   *
16545     11   ''
16546    118   ?
. . . . .
```

If you press CONT again you'll find we're getting into lines 1∅∅∅ onwards, which are cheerfully printing out where they themselves are stored! But that's not the best line of attack.

Try a few other programs in lines 1∅, 2∅, 3∅, etc. Leave lines 1∅∅∅–1∅4∅ as they are, and PEEK your programs using GOTO 1∅∅∅. You'll soon see the beginnings of patterns to the listing.

One thing that's obviously peculiar is the way *numbers* are stored. The 1∅ in PRINT AT ∅,1∅, for example, seems to occupy addresses 16534–16541. This looks a big space for such a small number; but it's related to the fact that the 1000 can handle *floating-point* arithmetic (decimals like 23.567) and use a code that is suitable. You can have hours of fun just trying to work out how a given number is actually stored.

But the real beauty of it all is that now you know *where* a given program byte lives, you can *change* it. The instruction that gives you this terrible power over the poor 1000 is

```
POKE
```

Let's see it in action.

What does our little program above do? It PRINTs out * at position ∅,1∅. RUN and see.

Let's POKE it. Add two program lines:

```
3∅ POKE 16544, 12
4∅ GOTO 1∅
```

Now run it by typing

```
GOTO   3∅
```

Instead of * you get £ printed out.

Why? Because line 3∅ POKEs into address 16544 (where the original * was stored) the new character with code 12, which is £.

If you ask the machine to LIST you'll find that line 2∅ of the original program now reads

```
2∅    PRINT AT ∅, 1∅; "£"
```

Let's experiment a little further. BREAK, and get rid of lines 3∅ and 4∅. Change line 2∅ back to its original form using EDIT. At the same time, change the ∅ to 1, so you have

```
2∅    PRINT AT 1, 1∅;"*"
```

Now GOTO 1∅∅∅ and PEEK it all again. Use CONT to carry on when you run out of screen.

You'll spot the change. Addresses 16526 and 16528 have become

```
16526     29    1
16528    129    ▟
```

Otherwise all is as before.

To test our new knowledge, add the following program lines.

```
3∅    POKE 16526, 29
4∅    POKE 16528, 129
5∅    GOTO 2∅
```

Change line 2∅ back to reading PRINT AT ∅,1∅;"*". Now press RUN.

The screen should display *two* asterisks, in screen lines ∅ and 1. It runs through the first program, printing on screen line ∅; then it POKEs the values needed for screen line 1; then GOTO 2∅ makes it PRINT again in the new line.

Try LIST; once more you'll find line 2∅ has become PRINT AT 1, 1∅;"*".

You can't POKE the ROM, of course—"Read only" means what it says! And a good job too, otherwise an accidental POKE might ruin the BASIC interpreter. In consequence, you can POKE fearlessly as the whim takes you, to see what happens.

The possibilities opened up by POKE are vast. But to handle it properly you need to know more about the detailed internal codes used by the 1000. Chapter 27 of the *Manual* gives the basic information you need. If you're keen enough, you can work the rest out using the PEEK routine above, lines 1∅∅∅–1∅4∅. I'm not going to say more, because it's better to work it out for yourself than to read through a complicated description given by someone else. But, as in the other sections of this book, I wanted to set your mind working along useful lines. By the time you've reached here, you'll have seen that PEEK and POKE are not the awful mystery that they are often made out to be. It's just that they dig deeper into the *system* by which the 1000 functions. Experiment with them: POKEing presents a fascinating challenge and a potentially rewarding one.

"Adam?"
"Yes, dear?"
"What's that fig-leaf for?"

# WHAT I HAVEN'T TOLD YOU ABOUT

Lots. Some of it is self-explanatory, like GOTO or FAST or SLOW. Some isn't, but there just isn't enough space: CLEAR, RAND, LIST, LLIST, vectors, arrays, etc. Some is downright complicated: the full story of PEEK and POKE stands out in this category. Consult the *Manual* for more information; and for USR see overpage: What Next?, regarding machine code. Sorry, I'd like to tell you more but there just isn't space for everything; and in any case this *is* an *introductory* book.

I also haven't told you in detail about the various functions like SIN, COS, TAN, ARCSIN, ARCCOS, ARCTAN, LN, EXP, ABS. I assume on the whole that if you need these, you'll know what they are; they're what you get on a scientific calculator. There are various restrictions on ranges of values; the *Manual* tells you most (but not, sadly, all) of these. Note that trig is done in *radians,* not degrees: X degrees is X*PI/18∅ radians and you have to tell that to the 1000. I don't think this book is the right place to teach you trigonometry.

A few of the program listings involve these functions, though. If you don't understand them, don't worry: *nobody has told this to the 1000.* You can still copy the listing, and see what happens. (I don't claim it's always easy: I doubt POKE would succumb to such analysis with any rapidity.) Nothing you type on the screen can do any harm to the 1000; the worst you can do is to get in a mess and have to start again.

So you've survived this far. Congratulations!
The question is,

# WHAT NEXT?

(1) Of course, there's the Timex *Manual*.

(2) In the United States there are a number of local usergroups, most of which publish their own newsletter. However, one of the best magazines in this country that users and prospective users of the Timex/Sinclair 1000 might avail themselves of is:

**SYNC** magazine

a bi-monthly magazine which carries complete application programs, tips and techniques for more effective programming, hardware modifications and in-depth evaluations of software, peripherals and books.

Subscriptions to **SYNC** cost $10.00 per year (6 issues). **SYNC,** 39 E. Hanover Ave., Morris Plains, NJ 07950. (201) 540-0445.

(3) There are local T/S 1000 and ZX81 Usergroups.

(4) One thing you *will* want is the 16K extension RAM. There were connection problems with early versions of this, and it's still not a good idea to move the 1000 + 16K RAM around while it's working, as you tend to lose stuff from memory. Don't let this put you off, though. One useful trick is to put extra solder on the "fingers" on the printed circuit board, where the 16K RAM plugs in. Another is to do what some engineers I know at GEC did—permanently solder the two units together! The only problem is that you can't then add on other stuff. Flexible wires soldered on, or special connectors, can help. There are also non-Sinclair RAMs; see the magazine.

(5) I don't recommend getting too carried away buying add-ons (other than the 16K RAM) for the 1000. The point is that if you want to spend a lot more cash, you'd do better to go on to a more sophisticated machine; one for which there are (or will be) features like color display, sound, disc storage—and possibly lightpens, paddles, high-resolution graphics, and a proper keyboard. The great charm of the 1000 is that it is cheap and that you can learn a lot from it: buying lots of add-ons adds to the expense.

(6) On the brainwork side: you're going to find BASIC a bit limited and clumsy after a while; and that means learning machine code. As well as the books mentioned in the Timex *Manual,* there's Tony Baker's *Mastering Machine Code on your ZX80 or ZX81,* we haven't actually seen a copy yet.

(7) By the time you feel like moving on to fancier equipment, the whole scene will have changed, given the pace at which it's moving. Buy a selection of magazines to keep in touch. Remember how the first pocket calculators cost about $300 and now they're giving them away with cornflakes? It's not quite like that with personal computers, but what's happening is that you get more and more features for the same money—say $500 or so. The trends will probably start to settle down within a year or two, but at the moment you need to shop around and compare different machines with a view to what you really think will be useful.

(8) Happy programming!

# PROGRAM LISTINGS

The programs that follow are intended to illustrate various features of the 1000, and to show you the sort of thing that can be achieved with 1K of memory. Each is complete in itself, and need only be copied and RUN. It's not necessary to understand the commands in the listing.

However, by the time you've worked your way through this book, you ought to be able to analyse the way these programs work. This won't always be easy, though: it's often difficult to get used to somebody else's programming style.

While on the subject of style: the restricted memory and some of the features of Sinclair BASIC have on occasion forced me to write the programs in ways which while efficient, are not as clear as a civilized program would be. Good style requires clarity, partly because it's a soul-destroying task trying to modify programs that look like *Finnegan's Wake* written in Chinese, and partly because you tend to make fewer errors anyway.

I have deliberately left a lot of programs with untidy line numbers. It's amazing how often errors creep in when you renumber a program. And I wanted to emphasize that you do *not* have to use line numbers that are multiples of 1∅. The only reasons for doing this, apart from fashion or fussiness, are to leave room for changes to the program, or for inserting tracers when debugging.

In these listings, I've drawn the graphic characters as they appear on the keyboard. Boxes around a letter, such as [H], mean inverse video; an open box □ denotes a space. Obvious spaces aren't made explicit; but ones that are important and easily missed out *are*.

The programs are not listed in any special order. Dip in!

For my first prepacked program, I chose one whose internal workings are pretty close to the surface. It calculates:

# THE AREA OF A TRIANGLE

If the sides of a triangle are a, b, c then its area is given by the formula $\sqrt{s(s - a)(s - b)(s - c)}$ where $s = \frac{1}{2}(a + b + c)$. This program uses the formula to compute the area of a triangle whose sides are INPUT in turn.

```
 1Ø   INPUT A
 2Ø   PRINT "A = □";A
 3Ø   INPUT B
 4Ø   PRINT "B = □";B
 5Ø   INPUT C
 6Ø   PRINT "C = □";C
 7Ø   LET S = .5*(A + B + C)
 75  LET X = S*(S - A)*(S - B)*(S - C)
 8Ø   IF X < Ø THEN GOTO 11Ø
 9Ø   PRINT "AREA IS □";SQR X
1ØØ   STOP
11Ø   PRINT "IMPOSSIBLE TO FORM A TRIANGLE"
```

PROGRAM NOTES

(1) Programs that evaluate formulae and print out the answers are so transparent that it would be cheating to count them as "real" programs! They're more like mechanized pocket calculator routines. But, at this stage, I felt that an obvious program wouldn't do any harm.

(2) You can easily modify this type of program to work out any reasonable formula. Perhaps this is one way to make mathematical formulae more interesting, and get some educational value out of the 1000. Here are a few suggestions for possible programs:

(a) The surface area of a sphere of radius r is $4\pi r^2$.
[$\pi$ is PI on the screen: key M in FUNCTION mode. That is, you press SHIFT with your left finger while pressing FUNCTION/ENTER with your right; then release SHIFT and press M.]

(b) The volume of a sphere of radius r is $\frac{4}{3}\pi r^3$.

(c) The volume of a cylinder of radius r and height h is $\pi r^2 h$.

(d) The volume of a cone of radius r and height h is $\frac{1}{3}\pi r^2 h$.

(e) The solutions of the quadratic equation $ax^2 + bx + c = 0$ are given by

$$x = (-b \pm \sqrt{}(b^2 - 4ac))/2a$$

(Work out the + and the − roots separately. If $b^2 - 4ac < 0$, the roots are imaginary, and you'll have to deal with this, either by PRINTing "IMAGINARY ROOTS" or concocting a piece of program to work them out if you know about complex numbers. You'll also have to deal with the possibility that $a = 0$.)

(f) The sum $1 + 4 + 9 + \ldots + n^2$ is equal to $\frac{1}{6}n(n + 1)(2n + 1)$. INPUT n and PRINT the sum. [Also, for comparison, work it out by summing the series, using FOR/NEXT, once you've read LOOPING, page 29.]

(g) The period of swing of a pendulum of length $l$ is $T = 2\pi\sqrt{}(l/g)$ where g is the acceleration due to gravity: 981 cm/sec/sec or 32 ft/sec/sec.

(h) In fact g varies from place to place: a more accurate approximation is that it depends on latitude L and height h above sea level, according to the formula

$$g = 980.616 - 2.5928 \cos(2L) + 0.0069\cos^2(2L) - 0.0003h \quad \text{cm/sec/sec}$$

Write a program to work out g, and T, given L, h, and $l$.

If triangles aren't your thing, why not write a program to work out your bank balance?

## AM I OVERDRAWN?

```
1Ø PRINT "PREVIOUS BALANCE IS □";
2Ø INPUT B
3Ø PRINT B
4Ø PRINT "LIST DEBITS"
5Ø INPUT D
6Ø IF D < Ø THEN GOTO 9Ø
7Ø LET B = B - D
```

```
 8Ø  GOTO 5Ø
 9Ø  PRINT "LIST CREDITS"
1ØØ  INPUT D
11Ø  IF D < Ø THEN GOTO 14Ø
12Ø  LET B = B + D
13Ø  GOTO 1ØØ
14Ø  PRINT "CURRENT BALANCE IS □";B
```

PROGRAM NOTES

(1) Lines 6Ø and 11Ø are *delimiters* (see page 39). If you input a negative number the machine knows you've finished the listing. (This negative number is *not* included in your bank balance!)
(2) Debits are mostly checkbook stub figures. But don't forget standing orders, (An obvious first improvement is to build these into the program, see if you can manage it) and withdrawals from cash-dispensers.
(3) Credits: don't forget your salary check! Maybe you can build this in too.
(4) Your younger children can play banks for hours using this.
(5) If you add two more lines:

```
 55  PRINT D
1Ø5  PRINT D
```

the machine will list the items. If you have more than 2Ø items the screen fills, and it is necessary to press CLS and then CONT to continue.

Mathematicians call this a "stochastic process". I still think it's fun.

## DRUNKARD

Imagine a particle sitting on a line. Every second it either moves one step left, or one right, at random. Mathematicians call this a random (or drunkard's) walk. What's surprising is that it moves around a lot, but generally pretty slowly. In theory it almost always reaches every point of the line, but takes infinitely long on average to get there!

Watch the drunkard and see how long he takes to reach the edge of the screen.

```
1Ø   LET T = Ø
2Ø   LET X = 3Ø
3Ø   PLOT X,Ø
4Ø   LET T = T + 1
5Ø   LET R = 2*RND
6Ø   IF R < 1 THEN LET X = X − 1
7Ø   IF R > = 1 THEN LET X = X + 1
8Ø   IF X < Ø OR X > 63 THEN GOTO 11Ø
9Ø   SCROLL
1ØØ  GOTO 3Ø
11Ø  PRINT AT Ø,Ø;T
```

PROGRAM NOTE

If you get fed up waiting, press BREAK; then PRINT AT Ø,Ø;T; then ENTER.

Here's a program to keep the kids quiet on a rainy afternoon . . .

## SINK THE BISMARCK

A routine patrol on the North Sea. . . . Suddenly, from out of the fog, the enemy vessel appears, about a mile away. You tell your gunners to set the elevation and muzzle velocity of their gun. Will you be able to sink the *Bismarck?*

```
1Ø   LETT = 15*(1 + RND)
2Ø   PRINT AT 21,Ø;
3Ø   FOR J = Ø TO 31
4Ø   PRINT "▀";
5Ø   NEXT J
6Ø   PRINT AT 2Ø,T − 2; "▄▙▙▄"
7Ø   PRINT AT 2,Ø; "E =";
8Ø   INPUT E
9Ø   PRINT E
```

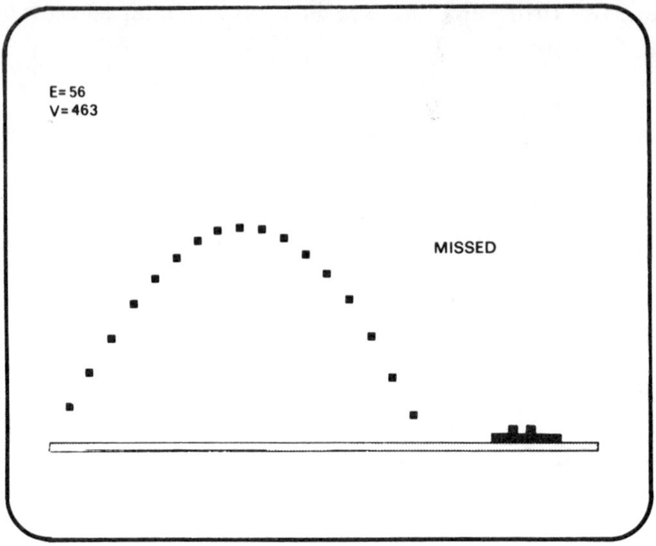


*Figure 17*

```
1ØØ  PRINT "V =";
11Ø  INPUT V
12Ø  PRINT V
13Ø  LET A = V*COS(PI*E/18Ø)
14Ø  LET B = V*SIN(PI*E/18Ø)
15Ø  FOR J = Ø TO B/16
16Ø  LET C = .Ø1*(B*J - 16*J*J)
17Ø  IF A*J > 62ØØ THEN GOTO 22Ø
18Ø  IF C > 4Ø THEN GOTO 2ØØ
19Ø  PLOT .Ø1*A*J,C + 2
2ØØ  NEXT J
21Ø  IF ABS(A*B/32ØØ - T) < 3 THEN GOTO 24Ø
22Ø  PRINT AT 1Ø,2Ø;"MISSED"
23Ø  STOP
24Ø  FOR J = Ø TO 5
25Ø  PRINT AT 2Ø - J, T - 2; "GLUG"
26Ø  NEXT J
```

PROGRAM NOTES



(1) It begins by drawing the sea, and a randomly placed silhouette of a ship. Line 1Ø chooses the random position, 2Ø–5Ø PRINT the sea, and 6Ø the ship.

(2) 7∅–13∅ INPUT and display the elevation E and muzzle velocity V. The player when asked by the machine, must INPUT these from the keyboard. E is in degrees, and must be between ∅° and 9∅°; V is in feet per second and must be positive.
(3) 13∅–2∅∅ compute and plot the trajectory of the shell at one-second intervals—see mathematical notes, below.
(4) 21∅ gives you a "HIT" if your shell hits the waterline within 6∅∅ feet of the ship's centre. Adjust the 3 to 2 or 1.5 for a more difficult game, or to 4 or 5 for an easier one.
(5) 22∅–26∅ are output routines for a HIT or MISS. The fancy HIT routine in 24∅–26∅ can lead to the program running out of memory (in harmless ways) and you can, if you prefer, replace it by the simpler

```
24∅   PRINT AT 1∅,2∅;"HIT"
```

and delete 25∅ and 26∅. Or delete the "sea", 2∅–5∅.
(6) To start or restart, hit RUN followed by ENTER, as usual. Incidentally, to stop the little dears hitting NEW and wiping out your laboriously entered program, you can make a cardboard template to sit over the keyboard, with only holes at keys they need to use. This is often a useful trick.
(7) The screen here is 64∅∅ feet wide, as simulated.
(8) The program is moderately "user-friendly" and goes on running even if the shell goes off the top of the screen (thanks to line 18∅).
(9) The graphics in line 4∅ are shifted S; in 6∅ shifted 6,W,W,6.
(10) "PI" in lines 13∅ and 14∅ is key M in function mode, *not* keys P and I!

### MATHEMATICAL NOTES

The shell's path is calculated using a mathematical formula accurate (in the absence of air resistance) for a body moving under gravity—assumed to be 32 ft/sec/sec. In line 15∅ J represents time; A is the horizontal component of velocity and B the vertical component; the PI*E/18∅ converts from degrees to radians. Line 16∅ computes the height at time J and converts to screen coordinates by dividing by 1∅∅. (Each PLOT pixel is 1∅∅ feet square.) In line 15∅, B/16 is the time taken to hit the waterline. In line 21∅, A*B/16∅∅ is the distance it has then gone; the 32∅∅ happens because we are using a PRINT statement in line 6∅, so the distance to the ship is 2∅∅*T.

If any other feature of the program puzzles you, try changing it and see what happens.

Notice that, while *playing* a computer game like this has only minor educational value (pressing the right key, judging distances and angles), *writing* or *understanding* it requires some knowledge of both programming and mathematics, and could be used to advantage as motivation either in the classroom or at home.

Here's a variation on the PLOT routine, producing some beautiful curves:

# LISSAJOUS FIGURES

These were invented by Nathaniel Bowditch in 1815, but named after Jules-Antoine Lissajous who reinvented them in 1857. They illustrate another way to PLOT interesting curves, using what mathematicians call a *parametrization*. What that means is that you make X and Y depend on a variable T, and PLOT X,Y for sequences of T's.

```
1∅   INPUT M
2∅   INPUT N
3∅   INPUT P
4∅   FOR J = ∅ TO 2∅∅
5∅   LET X = 3∅ + 3∅*SIN(P + M*PI*J/1∅∅)
6∅   LET Y = 2∅ + 2∅*SIN(N*PI*J/1∅∅)
7∅   PLOT X,Y
8∅   NEXT J
```

PROGRAM NOTES

(1) M and N should be whole numbers, not too large or memory runs out. Say M,N5 or less.
(2) P should be somewhere between ∅ and 2, say .3 or .7; though larger or negative P do no harm.
(3) A good start is M = 3, N = 5, P = .5.
(4) "PI" is key M in function mode.

The 1000 can do statistics, thanks to its random number generator RND. This program simulates

# MONOPOLY DICE

If you've played *Monopoly** you'll remember that to find out how far your piece moves you throw two dice, and add the result. You may also have noticed that the total 7 is more common than anything else. In fact, out of 36 throws of the dice you should expect the total

2 to happen on average 1 time
3 to happen on average 2 times
4 to happen on average 3 times
5 to happen on average 4 times
6 to happen on average 5 times
7 to happen on average 6 times
8 to happen on average 5 times
9 to happen on average 4 times
10 to happen on average 3 times
11 to happen on average 2 times
12 to happen on average 1 time.

Of course, you won't usually get those numbers exactly, but in the long run you should get close . . . on average!

You can use the 1000 to explore the world of statistics, by *simulating* this kind of thing using random numbers. This program "throws" two dice 144 times (4 times 36, to make life easy), counts how many times the total is 2, 3, 4, . . . etc.; plots out the results in a "bar chart"; and also compares the actual result with the expected theoretical numbers.

```
10  FAST
20  DIM A(11)
30  FOR J = 1 TO 144
40  LET D = 1 + INT(6*RND) + INT(6*RND)
50  LET A(D) = A(D) + 1
60  NEXT J
```

*'Monopoly' is a registered Trade Mark of Parker Brothers.

```
 7Ø   SLOW
 8Ø   FOR J = 2 TO 12
 9Ø   FOR T = Ø TO 2*(6 − ABS(7 − J))
1ØØ   PLOT 6 + 4*J,2*T
11Ø   NEXT T
12Ø   FOR T = Ø TO A(J − 1)
13Ø   PLOT 8 + 4*J,T
14Ø   NEXT T
15Ø   NEXT J
```

## PROGRAM NOTES

(1) FAST/SLOW speeds the calculation up but gives the PLOT step by step.

(2) The bar chart shows the theoretical number as a dotted bar, the "experimental" one as a solid bar; the bars from left to right represent totals of 2, 3, 4, . . ., 12.

## PROJECT

Write 2, 3, 4, . . ., 12 under the right bars as part of the program. Allow the length of run (here 144) to be varied according to an INPUT variable. (Careful with the "theoretical" numbers.)

Repeat the whole run a fixed number of times, say 1Ø, and take the average number of occurrences of each total before plotting.

Even a short program can produce intriguing results. You'll see why this one is called

# BILLIARD BOUNCE

```
 1Ø   FOR I = Ø TO 32Ø
 2Ø   LET A = I − 128*INT(I/128)
 3Ø   LET B = I − 40*INT(I/40)
 4Ø   LET A = 63.5 − ABS(A − 63.5)
 5Ø   LET B = 19.5 − ABS(B − 19.5) +22
 6Ø   PLOT A,B
7ØØ   NEXT I
```

PROGRAM NOTE

Two mathematical tricks have been used to make the ball bounce. You don't need to worry about them but, for the record, here they are. We imagine the billiard ball moving off along a diagonal line at an angle of 45° to the horizontal. The position is then converted to one inside a rectangle of size 128 × 4Ø by using lines 5Ø and 6Ø to reduce the horizontal coordinate modulo 128 and the vertical modulo 4Ø. This rectangle is then folded in half, vertically and horizontally, by lines 7Ø and 8Ø—just like a piece of paper folded twice, once in each direction. The folds create the bounce effect at edges.

---

Here's an example of an "educational" program. To fit into 1K I've had to be less ambitious, but the flavor is there:

---

# ARITHMETIC TEST

This program sets the operator (your seven-year-old) an addition sum involving two random two-digit numbers; checks if his answer is wrong or right; and, if wrong, explains how to get it right.

```
 1Ø  LET V = VAL "1Ø"
 2Ø  LET C = Ø
 3Ø  PRINT "HI. IM ZX81. WHO ARE YOU?"
 4Ø  INPUT E$
 5Ø  PRINT "OK,□";E$;"□ CAN YOU ANSWER"
 6Ø  PRINT "THIS?"
 7Ø  LET X = INT(V*V*RND)
 8Ø  LET Y = INT(V*V*RND)
 9Ø  IF X + Y < = 12 THEN GOTO 7*V
1ØØ  LET X1 = INT(X/V)
11Ø  LET X2 = X - V*X1
12Ø  LET Y1 = INT(Y/V)
13Ø  LET Y2 = Y - V*Y1
14Ø  IF X2 + Y2 > = V THEN LET C = 1
15Ø  PRINT X;"+";Y;"□ = □?□";
```

```
16Ø  INPUT A
17Ø  PRINT A; "□?"
18Ø  LET B = X + Y - A
19Ø  PRINT ("RIGHT" AND B = Ø) + ("SORRY, WRONG" AND
          B <> Ø)
2ØØ  IF B = Ø THEN GOTO 19Ø
21Ø  PRINT X2;"+";Y2;"□ IS □";X2 + Y2 - C*V;
22Ø  IF C = 1 THEN PRINT "□ CARRY 1"
23Ø  PRINT "□ AND THEN □";X1;"+";Y1;"+ THE CARRY"
          AND C = 1; "□ IS □";X1 + Y1 + C
24Ø  PRINT "GIVING □";X + Y
```

## PROGRAM NOTES

(1) Line 1Ø is a space-saving dodge. Because of the way the 1000 does arithmetic, integer constants take less space if stored as VAL "n" rather than plain n. Funny, isn't it? If you use a constant more than about four times (to compensate for the VAL storage space) it's worth using this method when space is tight. The disadvantage is that it makes programs less than transparent, and we haven't used it much.

(2) Line 3Ø is a confidence-builder. It asks the operator for his name. Line 5Ø uses the name to ask a question.

(3) Line 16Ø is where the operator tells the computer what he thinks the answer is.

(4) Lines 2ØØ onwards explain to the operator how the sum should have been done, if he got it wrong.

(5) The main difficulty in "educational" programs of this kind is that they tend to require lengthy displays of text, which eats storage space. This program could be much improved given more space — for example, setting various levels of difficulty, giving more advice if something goes wrong with the operator's calculation, protecting the program better against the operator pressing wrong keys by mistake, and so forth. And, of course, more interesting sums than plain addition would be an improvement. If you buy the 16K RAM you can do a lot better. But most of the basic principles show up in this little program.

You can also buy prepacked "educational" programs, advertised in the magazines. The quality of these varies hugely, and some are not as good as mine!



(6) A good program wouldn't need to be RUN each time, but would ask the operator if he wanted another go, and if he said yes, RUN

automatically. It's easy to add a few lines to achieve this—but not in 1K of memory!

---

Here's a simple exercise in moving graphics, using that "invisible border". If you run it you'll see why it's called:

---

# MACY'S

```
 1Ø  FOR U = 2 TO 32 STEP 1Ø
 2Ø  FOR V = Ø TO 19
 3Ø  PLOT V,U
 4Ø  NEXT V
 5Ø  NEXT U
 6Ø  LET G = 17
 7Ø  LET I = 17
 8Ø  GOSUB 2ØØ
1ØØ  IF INKEY$ <> ""THEN GOTO 1ØØ
11Ø  IF INKEY$ = "" THEN GOTO 11Ø
115  IF INKEY$ > "4" THEN GOTO 1ØØ
12Ø  LET F = 22 - 5*VAL INKEY$
125  IF F = G THEN GOTO 1ØØ
13Ø  FOR I = G TO F STEP SGN(F - G)
14Ø  GOSUB 2ØØ
15Ø  NEXT I
16Ø  LET G = F
17Ø  GOTO 1ØØ
2ØØ  PRINT AT I,1Ø;"□ □";AT I + 1,1Ø;"▛▜";AT I + 2,
     1Ø;"▌□▐";AT I + 3,1Ø;"▙▟";AT I + 4,1Ø;"□ □"
21Ø  RETURN
```

PROGRAM NOTES

(1) The horizontal lines plotted in 1Ø–5Ø are floors in Macy's store. The black box (subroutine in line 2ØØ) is a lift. If you input a floor number (1, 2, 3, or 4) the lift will move to the chosen floor.

(2) To protect against inputs over 4, line 115 has been added. Unfortunately other protection overloads the memory, with 1K.

(3) The lift only moves up and down; so line 2ØØ has an invisible border at the top and bottom only.

An example of text-display:

# PARTRIDGE PRINTOUT

This yuletide program displays, at singable speed, the words to a well-known carol.

```
 1∅  FOR D = 1 TO 12
 2∅  PAUSE 45*D + 25∅
 2∅  CLS
 4∅  PRINT "ON THE □";D;
 5∅  IF D = 1 THEN PRINT "ST";
 6∅  IF D = 2 THEN PRINT "ND";
 7∅  IF D > 2 THEN PRINT "TH";
 8∅  PRINT "□DAY OF CHRISTMAS MY □□ TRUE LOVE
        GAVE TO ME"
 9∅  GOSUB 132 - D
1∅∅  NEXT D
11∅  STOP
12∅  PRINT "12 DRUMMERS DRUMMING"
121  PRINT "11 PIPERS PIPING"
122  PRINT "1∅ LORDS A-LEAPING"
123  PRINT "9 LADIES DANCING"
124  PRINT "8 MAIDS A-MILKING"
125  PRINT "7 SWANS A-SWIMMING"
126  PRINT "6 GEESE A-LAYING"
127  PRINT "5 GOLD RINGS"
128  PRINT "4 CALLING BIRDS"
129  PRINT "3 FRENCH HENS"
13∅  PRINT "2 TURTLE DOVES AND"
131  PRINT "A PARTRIDGE IN A PEAR TREE"
14∅  RETURN
```

PROGRAM NOTES

(1) The screen blanks out for a few seconds before anything happens.

(2) Line 2∅ adjusts the tempo. The 45 adjusts the time for lines 12∅–131; the 25∅ the time for 4∅–8∅. Boxes denote important (non-obvious) spaces.

(3) The daft machine prints "3TH" instead of "3RD". You can obviously fix this by changing line 7∅ to

```
7∅   IF D > 3 THEN PRINT "TH";
```

and adding

```
65   IF D = 3 THEN PRINT "RD";
```

but if you do this, you'll find it grinds to a halt just before the end of the verses with a report code 4/something. It won't, with this change, run on 1K of RAM. The large amount of text makes storage problems acute; in fact, the program as listed terminates with a report 4/100, meaning it didn't quite execute the whole thing; but it just squeezes in the last line of text. I had some fun trimming the program to run at all on 1k. Maybe you can do better, though:

### PROJECT 1

Improve the program so that it prints "3RD" where it should, displays in singable time (you can't just omit 2∅ or change it to, say PAUSE 5∅∅, which bores everyone reading it), and runs on 1K of memory, in BASIC. No cheating with machine code!

### PROJECT 2

Change the words to get a Programmer's Carol, with lines like, say, 1∅ LOGS A-LOOPING, 5 MICRO CHIPS, 2 SUBTLE BUGS.

There's a mole hidden in the hundred-acre wood. Can you find him?

# MOLEHUNT

```
1∅   LET I = INT(1∅*RND)*2 + 21
2∅   LET J = INT(1∅*RND)*2 + 12
3∅   LET N = ∅
4∅   PRINT AT 18,∅;"FIND ME"
5∅   INPUT A
6∅   LET N = N + 1
```

```
 7∅   PRINT AT 19,∅;A;"□"
 8∅   INPUT B
 9∅   PRINT AT 2∅,∅;B;"□"
1∅∅   LET A = 2*A + 19
11∅   LET B = 2*B + 1∅
12∅   PLOT A,B
13∅   LET G = (A − I)*(A − I) + (B − J)*(B − J)
14∅   IF G = ∅ THEN PRINT AT 21,∅;"GOT ME IN □";N
15∅   IF G > ∅ AND G < 25 THEN PRINT AT 21,∅;"WARM"
16∅   IF G > = 25 THEN PRINT AT 21,∅;"COLD"
21∅   GOTO 5∅
```

PROGRAM NOTES

(1) A and B are respectively horizontal and vertical coordinates in the 1∅∅-acre wood, and run from 1 to 1∅.

(2) The borders of the wood give a rectangle in the middle of the screen; memory prohibits drawing them, but as you dig holes (input A and B) you'll see whereabouts the wood is.

(3) G measures how close to the mole you are; the program uses this to tell you if you're close (WARM), way off (COLD), or spot on (GOT ME IN 723 or however many tries you took). You can change these messages to suit your personal taste (e.g. "OOPS THAT WAS CLOSE", "YAH, MISSED" AND "YEEEEOWWWCH").

(4) While this looks like a silly game, you can use it to teach the kids about coordinates. You may need to display the mole to begin with: an extra line

```
25   PLOT I,J
```

will do this.

The 1000, on FAST mode, is quite an effective number-cruncher. To convince you of this, take an 8-digit number and see how quickly this program will give its

# PRIME FACTORS

```
  1∅  INPUT K
  2∅  FAST
  3∅  PRINT K;"□ = □";
  4∅  LET K∅ = K
  5∅  IF INT(K/2)*2 = K THEN GOTO 14∅
  6∅  LET N = 3
  7∅  IF INT(K/N)*N ∞ K THEN GOTO 11∅
  8∅  IF N*N > K THEN GOTO 17∅
  9∅  LET N = N + 2
 1∅∅  GOTO 7∅
 11∅  PRINT N;".";
 12∅  LET K = K/N
 13∅  GOTO 7∅
 14∅  PRINT "2.";
 15∅  LET K = K/2
 16∅  GOTO 5∅
 17∅  IF K = K∅ THEN PRINT "[P][R][I][M][E]"
 18∅  IF K < K∅ AND K > 1 THEN PRINT K
 19∅  SLOW
```

PROGRAM NOTES

(1) INT(K/N)*N = K if and only if K is divisible by N. So this tests for divisors.

(2) The program tries dividing K by 2, and all odd numbers less than the square root of K. If no such divide K, then it is prime.

(3) If a divisor is found, the program divides K by it, and hunts for a new divisor of the same size. If it doesn't find one it looks for a bigger divisor.

(4) FAST means you only see the final output, which takes about 35 seconds with an 8-digit prime and less otherwise. If you delete line 2∅ it takes about 2 minutes and 2∅ seconds. The final SLOW is just to save resetting the machine later: always a civilized act! (The times quoted are for 11111117; obviously, they will change for different numbers.)

(5) Modifications: Embed this in a loop, and use a SCROLL instruction to produce a display of prime factors of K, K + 1, K + 2, . . . and so on indefinitely. (Delete the FAST, or the screen goes mad.)
(6) K has to be at most 8 digits, because the 1000 won't handle larger numbers with enough precision.
(7) This program could be made mathematically more efficient, for instance by excluding multiples of 3 or 5 from trial divisors. Can you use this to make a program run *faster?* The price for mathematical efficiency is increased program size: does the gain wipe out the loss if you're careful?

Everybody has programs to solve quadratic equations. What about this?

## SOLVING CUBICS

This program finds all real roots of cubic equations $ax^3 + bx^2 + cx + d = 0$, to reasonable accuracy.

```
 1Ø  INPUT A
 2Ø  INPUT B
 3Ø  INPUT C
 4Ø  INPUT D
 5Ø  LET B = B/A
 6Ø  LET C = C/A
 7Ø  LET D = D/A
 8Ø  LET X = Ø
 9Ø  LET G = 2*X*X*X + B*X*X - D
1ØØ  LET H = 3*X*X + 2*B*X + C
11Ø  IF H = Ø THEN GOTO 2ØØ
12Ø  IF ABS(X - (G/H)) < 1.E - 8 THEN GOTO 3ØØ
13Ø  LET X = G/H
14Ø  GOTO 9Ø
2ØØ  LET X = X + 1
21Ø  GOTO 9Ø
3ØØ  PRINT "X1 = □";X
4ØØ  LET A = B + X
41Ø  LET B = X*X + B*X + C
```

```
42Ø   LET D = A*A − 4*B
43Ø   IF D < Ø THEN PRINT "OTHERS IMAGINARY"
44Ø   IF ABS D < 1.E − 7 THEN PRINT "NUMERICAL
      INSTABILITY POSSIBLE"
445   IF D < △ THEN STOP
45Ø   PRINT "X2 = □";(− A + SQR D)/2
46Ø   PRINT "X3 = □";(− A − SQR D)/2
```

## PROGRAM NOTES

(1) The program finds one root of the equation by an iterative process known as the *Newton-Raphson method,* which involves taking a trial value for X and improving it successively until it gets near enough to a root. Lines 9Ø–15Ø perform this process.

(2) If you want to see the way this iteration works, add

```
131   PRINT X
```

and watch the numbers converge on the answer.

(3) Having found one root, the program divides out by this to get a quadratic and solves it by formula in lines 4ØØ–46Ø.

(4) If this quadratic has no real roots, line 43Ø applies; the program then crashes in line 45Ø but no harm is done.

(5) A fine point: for some cubics inaccuracies in the arithmetic build up too much, and the program may claim "OTHERS IMAGINARY" when this is not in fact the case. Line 44Ø warns the operator that this is on the cards. The problem is that the sign of D is crucial, and if D is close to Ø, errors can have a disastrous effect.

Most numerical methods encounter similar problems, and a large part of the subject called numerical analysis spends a lot of time tackling these.

(6) For example, try INPUTting A = 4, B = − 8, C = 5, D = − 51. You should get X1 = 3, other imaginary. Now try A = 4, B = − 16, C = − 5, D = 51: this time you get X1 = 3, X2 = 2.62132Ø3, X3 = − 1.62132Ø3.

# FRUIT MACHINE

```
  1Ø   LET C = Ø
  2Ø   DIM A(3)
  3Ø   FOR T = 1 TO 3
  4Ø   LET R = INT(3*RND)
  5Ø   LET A(T) = R
  6Ø   LET I = 5
  7Ø   LET J = 10*T - 5
  8Ø   GOSUB 1ØØ*R + 2ØØ
  9Ø   NEXT T
 1ØØ   LET C = C - 1
 11Ø   IF A(1) = A(2) AND A(2) = A(3) THEN GOTO 7ØØ
 12Ø   GOSUB 1ØØØ
 13Ø   INPUT B$
 14Ø   IF B$ = "S" THEN STOP
 15Ø   GOTO 3Ø
 2ØØ   PRINT AT I,J;"■■";AT I + 1,J;"■■"
 21Ø   RETURN
 3ØØ   PRINT AT I,J;"▚▚";AT I + 1,J;"▚▚"
 31Ø   RETURN
 4ØØ   PRINT AT I,J;"▒▓";AT I + 1,J;"▒▓"
 41Ø   RETURN
 7ØØ   LET C = C + 9
 72Ø   GOTO 12Ø
1ØØØ   IF C > = Ø THEN PRINT AT 18,5;"YOU HAVE WON
       □";C;"□DOLLARS□"
1Ø1Ø   IF C < Ø THEN PRINT AT 18,5;"YOU HAVE
       LOST □";-C; "□ DOLLARS"
1Ø1Ø   RETURN
```

PROGRAM NOTES

(1) This displays three decorated squares. If they are all the same, you win $9. If not, you lose $1. To play, push any key except "STOP" or "S"—we recommend ENTER as it saves a keystroke. Push "S" to stop.

(2) On average, you should break even. This is better than you'll get in the local pub.

(3) Note the use of subroutines to plot the three possible types of square.

(4) Note the proper use of the screen: you get a reasonable display in the middle, not a tiny little one bunched up in a corner.

The 1000 will let you call a subroutine from inside itself. This is known as recursive programming. See if you can work out how this program does its job:

## OBSCURE FACTORIALS

```
 1Ø  LET F = 1
 2Ø  INPUT N
 3Ø  FAST
 35  LET M = N
 4Ø  GOSUB 1ØØ
 5Ø  PRINT M;"□FACTORIAL IS□";F
 6Ø  SLOW
 7Ø  STOP
1ØØ  IF N < = 1 THEN RETURN  ┐
11Ø  LET F = F*N              │
12Ø  LET N = N - 1            ├─ subroutine
13Ø  GOSUB 1ØØ                │
14Ø  RETURN                   ┘
```

What day of the week were you born on? What day did Anne Boleyn die? Now you can find out with the:

## DAYFINDER

This program accepts as input a date D.M.Y. where D is the day number, M the month, and Y the year (e.g. 23.7.1066) and works out which day it is (was, will be).

```
1Ø   LET A$ = "033614625035"
2Ø   LET B$ = "SUNMONTUEWEDTHUFRISAT"
3Ø   INPUT D
4Ø   PRINT D;".";
5Ø   INPUT M
6Ø   PRINT M;".";
7Ø   INPUT Y
8Ø   PRINT Y;"□IS□";
9Ø   LET Z = Y - 1
1ØØ  LET C = INT(Z/4) - INT(Z/1ØØ) + INT(Z/4ØØ)
11Ø  LET X = Y + D + C + VAL A$(M) - 1
12Ø  IF M > 2 AND (Y = 4*INT(Y/4) AND Y <>
     1ØØ*INT(Y/1ØØ) OR
     Y = 4ØØ*INT(Y/4ØØ)) THEN LET X = X + 1
13Ø  LET X = X - 7*INT(X/7)
14Ø  PRINT B$(3*X + 1 TO 3*X + 3)
```

## PROGRAM NOTES

(1) Line 1Ø stores a list of twelve "monthly correction numbers" in compact form as a string. Line 1ØØ works out the month in the list as part of a computation explained in note (4).

(2) Line 2Ø uses a similar trick to simplify the printing routine. See how line 12Ø selects the right group of three letters.

(3) Line 1ØØ computes how many leap years have elapsed since the year dot. Remember: multiples of 4 are leap years, but multiples of 1ØØ are not unless also multiples of 4ØØ.

(4) Line 11Ø is the guts of the computation. The idea is to count the number of days elapsed since some (essentially arbitrary) reference date, but to save space by throwing away multiples of 7 since these won't affect the day of the week. So the number of years, Y, gets multiplied by 365; but 365 = 7*52 + 1 so instead of 365*Y we use Y. The curiosities of month-lengths are taken care of by A$(M). Note the use of VAL to convert a single-digit character to an actual *number*. To calibrate the program I chose a date for which we knew the day of the week—30.9. 1981 was a Wednesday—and that gave me the—1 correction on the end. Line 12Ø adjusts the computation in January or February of a Leap Year, where it would otherwise go wrong.



(5) One calendric subtlety is missing. In 1752 Britain changed from the "Old Style" calendar to the "New Style". The day after 2.9.1752 was 14.9.1752. My program assumes New Style.

Modify it to work with Old Style dates for pre-1752 periods.

(6) The program accepts impossible dates like −37.12.−992. Modify it to accept only sensible dates.

(7) It won't work for dates BC. Modify it so it will. NB: There was no year Ø between 1 BC and 1 AD, even if logically there should have been!

Another technique for moving graphics is the SCROLL command. Here it is used in conjunction with some string manipulation:

## THISISASINECURVE

```
1Ø   LET A$ = "THISISASINECURVE"
2Ø   LET T = Ø
3Ø   LET C = 15 + 15*SIN(T/1Ø)
4Ø   LET Q = T - 16*INT(T/16) + 1
5Ø   PRINT AT 21,C;A$(Q)
6Ø   SCROLL
7Ø   SCROLL
8Ø   LET T = T + 1
9Ø   GOTO 3Ø
```

What is it?

Exactly.

For a clearer picture, change T/1Ø in line 3Ø to T/3.

Strings and numbers are sometimes closer than you might imagine – for example, in:

# BINARY/DECIMAL CONVERSION

Binary numbers only use ∅'s and 1's; instead of ∅, 1, 2, 3, 4, 5, 6, . . . they go ∅, 1, 1∅, 11, 1∅∅, 1∅1, 11∅, . . . where in general something like 11∅1∅∅1 is worked out from right to left as

$$1 \times 1 + \varnothing \times 2 + \varnothing \times 4 + 1 \times 8 + \varnothing \times 16 + 1 \times 32 + 1 \times 64 = 1\varnothing 5$$

each digit counting double what the previous one does. Computers, of course, use binary numbers for internal work (though modern computers use sophisticated variants, in practice).

The following two programs convert an INPUT number from binary to decimal, or conversely.

BINARY TO DECIMAL

```
1∅   INPUT A$
2∅   PRINT A$;
3∅   LET L = LEN A$
4∅   LET S = VAL A$(1)
5∅   FOR J = 2 TO L
6∅   LET S = 2*S + VAL A$(J)
7∅   NEXT J
8∅   PRINT "□ IS □";S;"□ IN DECIMAL"
```

DECIMAL TO BINARY

```
 1∅   LET C$ = ""
 2∅   INPUT A
 3∅   PRINT A;
 4∅   LET D = INT(A/2)
 5∅   LET R = A - 2*D
 6∅   IF R = ∅ THEN LET B$ = "∅"
 7∅   IF R = 1 THEN LET B$ = "1"
 8∅   LET C$ = B$ + C$
 9∅   IF D = ∅ THEN GOTO 12∅
1∅∅   LET A = D
```

```
110  GOTO 40
120  PRINT "□ IS □";C$;"□ IN BINARY"
```

PROGRAM NOTES

(1) The INPUT for binary/decimal conversion must be a sequence of Ø's and 1's, like 11ØØØ1Ø1Ø11. For decimal/binary it must be a whole number, like 3427ØØ6.
(2) The two programs have been written to illustrate different approaches to the conversion problem. It would be possible to make both look very similar in structure.
(3) In the decimal/binary conversion, note that lines 6Ø–7Ø *cannot* be replaced by

```
60  LET B$ = "R"
```

You can avoid having two lines by using CHR$ and being clever; or you can write

```
60  LET B$ = ("1" AND R) + ("0" AND 1 - R)
```

which works for reasons to do with how the 1000 handles logic.

Or, yet again:

```
60  LET B$ = "0"
70  IF R = 1 THEN LET B$ = "1"
```

will do the trick and save a little space.

This program is designed so that Dad can set it up, and get twenty minutes' peace while the kids run it:

# HANGMAN WITH FATHERLY INPUT



In the game of *Hangman*, players guess letters in a secretly chosen word. Correct letters are written into their proper positions; wrong letters lose a life. Lose too many lives and you're dead. In this version one player (usually Dad) inputs five words while the other players aren't looking; then leaves them to play against the machine.

```
1Ø   DIM W$(5,12)
2Ø   FOR I = 1 TO 5
3Ø   INPUT W$(I)
4Ø   NEXT I
5Ø   FOR I = 1 TO 5
51   LET C$ = ""
52   FOR L = 1 TO 12
53   IF W$(I,L) = "□" THEN GOTO 55
54   NEXT L
55   LET L = L - 1
61   FOR P = 1 TO L
62   LET C$ = C$ + "-"
63   NEXT P
7Ø   LET N = 6
8Ø   PRINT AT 2,Ø;N, "LIVES"
85   IF N = Ø THEN GOTO 225
9Ø   INPUT G$
95   LET F = 1
1ØØ  FOR P = 1 TO L
11Ø  IF W$(I,P) <> G$ THEN GOTO 15Ø
12Ø  LET C$(P) = G$
13Ø  LET F = Ø
15Ø  NEXT P
16Ø  PRINT AT 11,11;C$
17Ø  LET N = N - F
19Ø  FOR P = 1 TO L
2ØØ  IF C$(P) = "-" THEN GOTO 8Ø
21Ø  NEXT P
22Ø  PRINT AT 15,Ø;"WIN"
225  PRINT AT 11,11;W$(I)
23Ø  INPUT C$
235  CLS
24Ø  NEXT I
```

## PROGRAM NOTES



(1) In lines 1Ø–4Ø Dad inputs five words of 12 or fewer letters. Having done this, he can go away and snooze until the program run ends.

(2) Guesses at letters are input from the keyboard. Correct letters are printed out in the center; incorrect ones lose a life. The game continues until all letters are guessed, or all lives lost; the machine then prints out the word concerned.
(3) The number of lives is 6; to change this alter line 7Ø. For example, for 1Ø lives (and a longer snooze) use 7Ø LET N = 1Ø.
(4) After each game, start the next by hitting ENTER.
(5) If you have the 16K RAM you can improve the program in several ways. (a) Input more words by changing the 5 in lines 1Ø, 2Ø and 5Ø to something bigger. (b) Protect against children inputting more than one letter, or nothing at all, by adding

```
91   IF G$ = "" THEN GOTO 9Ø
```

and changing G$ in lines 11Ø, 12Ø to G$(1).

This one is a good example of moving graphics:

# BRICKBAT

Bricks drop from the sky. If you catch them with your bat, they vanish. If you miss they pile up. When the piles get too high, you lose. How long can you survive?

```
1Ø   LET H = 11
3Ø   DIM A(4)
4Ø   LET P = INT(4*RND) + 1
6Ø   LET J = 5*P
7Ø   FOR I = 8 TO 21 − A(P)
8Ø   PRINT AT I,J;"▒"
81   PRINT AT I − 1,J;"□"
9Ø   LET M$ = INKEY$
1ØØ  IF M$ = "5" THEN LET H = H − 1
11Ø  IF M$ = "8" THEN LET H = H + 1
115  PRINT AT 15,H;"□■■■□"
12Ø  IF I = 15 AND ABS(H + 2 − J) < = 1 THEN GOTO 4Ø
125  NEXT I
13Ø  LET A(P) = A(P) + 1
```

```
135  IF A(P) = 7 THEN STOP
14Ø  GOTO 4Ø
```

PROGRAM NOTES

(1) Although this is a short listing, the graphic display uses a lot of memory, and the program only just fits into 1K. With the 16K RAM you can drop more columns of bricks (change the 4's in lines 3Ø, 4Ø) from a greater height (change the 8 in line 7Ø to Ø).
(2) To move the bat left or right use keys 5 and 8 (arrows give direction). For memory reasons, the program is *not* protected against the bat going off screen, so be careful.
(3) With 16K of RAM you count how many bricks have been dropped and how many missed, and print these numbers out as a score. In 1K *you* have to count the number of bricks in the piles at the end; or you can command the machine to PRINT A(1) + A(2) + A(3) + A(4).

At Harold Hustler's Vegas Venue they don't play ordinary roulette; they play

# LINETTE

This is roulette played in a straight line.

```
1Ø   LET W = 1ØØ
2Ø   INPUT B$
22   CLS
26   INPUT A
27   LET W = W − A
11Ø  FOR N = Ø TO 9
12Ø  PRINT AT 1Ø,2*N + 6;CHR$(28 + N)
13Ø  NEXT N
14Ø  LET R = INT(RND*5) + 5
15Ø  LET D = INT(RND*1Ø)
155  LET R = R*1Ø + D
16Ø  FOR N = Ø TO R
165  LET X = N − 1Ø*INT(N/1Ø)
```

```
17Ø   PRINT AT 1Ø,2*X + 6;CHR$ 128
18Ø   PRINT AT 1Ø,2*X + 6;CHR$(28 + X)
19Ø   NEXT N
2ØØ   PRINT At 1Ø,2*X + 6;CHR$(156 + X)
21Ø   GOTO 1Ø*CODE B$(1)
37Ø   IF VAL B$(1) = D THEN LET W = W + 1Ø*A
38Ø   GOTO 6ØØ
42Ø   IF INT(D/2) = D/2 THEN LET W = W + 2*A
43Ø   GOTO 6ØØ
52Ø   IF INT(D/2) <> D/2 THEN LET W = W + 2*A
6ØØ   PRINT AT 16,9;W;"□CHIPS"
61Ø   IF W > = Ø THEN GOTO 2Ø
62Ø   PRINT "HARRY''''S MOB WILL BE ROUND IN THE
          MORNING"
```

PROGRAM NOTES

(1) After RUN, you can bet either on EVEN, ODD, or a number between Ø and 9, by typing in your bet. (Any word starting E will be read as "even", anything starting O as "odd".)

(2) You then say how much you are betting by inputting a number. You start with $100, set in line 1Ø.

(3) If you win you get back twice the stake on E or O; ten times the stake on a number. This theoretically makes it a "fair" game.

(4) You can bet more than you have in the kitty; but beware if you lose!

(5) In line 62Ø there is *no* space in THEMORNING. Why? Put one in and see. ''''is a *single* character (shifted Q).

(6) To stop, on a character input, hit DELETE and then STOP. On a numerical input STOP will do.

# T/S-WORD ANSWERS

**Across**

2. At
7. Basic program
12. Orate
13. One
15. Trigonometrical
16. Spaced
18. Holds
19. Silex
20. Accurately
21. Assign
23. Entries
24. Or
27. Primal
29. Smacks
31. Ada
33. Traced
34. Even lines
35. Go
39. Data entry
40. Thing
41. Potent
42. Loops

**Down**

1. Matrix
3. Tuna
4. Compute
5. Pascal triangle
6. Read
7. Batch
8. Still
9. Chooses
10. Roots
11. Gremlin
13. Octal numbering
14. Electric plug
17. True
22. In addition
30. Sin
32. Best bit
36. Oddly
37. Bytes
38. Atom

# PROGRAM INDEX

# INDEX